Simple Prayers & Blessings

Inspirations for the New Millennium

MARGARET ANNE HUFFMAN
GARY WILDE

All rights reserved under International and Pan American copyright conventions. Copyright © 1999 Publications International, Ltd. This publication may not be reproduced or quoted in whole or in part by any means whatsoever without written permission from Louis Weber, C.E.O. of Publications International, Ltd., 7373 North Cicero Avenue, Lincolnwood, Illinois 60646. Permission is never granted for commercial purposes. Printed in U.S.A.

PUBLICATIONS INTERNATIONAL, LTD.

Margaret Anne Huffman is an award-winning journalist and former family/lifestyle editor of *The Shelbyville News*. She has also written and contributed to 17 books. Her most recent titles include *A Moment With God for Mothers* and *Through the Valley: Prayers for Violent Times*.

Gary Wilde is a full-time freelance author and editor who has written numerous books, educational materials, and magazine articles on religious and self-help issues. He is the author of *The Bedside Book of Prayer: Devotions for Daily Life* and editor of the devotional quarterly *Quiet Hour*.

Cover Photo: Carr Cliffton © 1998

Quotations selected by Kacy Gramckow.

Page 14: Excerpt from *Letters to Malcolm: Chiefly on Prayer* by C.S. Lewis, copyright © 1964, 1963 by C.S. Lewis PTE, Ltd. and renewed 1992, 1991 by Arthur Owen Barfield, reprinted by permission of Harcourt Brace & Company. **Page 36:** From *Till Armageddon: A Perspective on Suffering* by Billy Graham, © 1981, Word Publishing, Nashville, Tennessee. All rights reserved. **Page 66:** From *The Collected Verse of Edgar A. Guest* by Edgar A. Guest, © 1984. Used with permission of NTC/Contemporary Publishing Company. **Page 74:** From *Another Day* by Eugenia Price. Copyright © 1984 by Eugenia Price. Used by permission of Doubleday, a division of Bantam Doubleday Dell Publishing Group, Inc. *Page 96:* From *Till Armageddon: A Perspective on Suffering* by Billy Graham, © 1981, Word Publishing, Nashville, Tennessee. All rights reserved. **Page 124:** From *Answers to Life's Problems* by Billy Graham, © 1960, 1988, Word Publishing, Nashville, Tennessee. All rights reserved. **Page 126:** From *Mother Teresa: A Simple Path* compiled by Lucinda Vardey; published by Rider. **Page 142:** Excerpt from *The Sign of Jonas* by Thomas Merton, copyright 1953 by The Abbey of Our Lady of Gethsemani and renewed 1981 by the Trustees of the Merton Legacy Trust, reprinted by permission of Harcourt Brace & Company. **Page 176:** Taken from *15 Minutes Alone with God* by Emilie Barnes, copyright © 1994 by Harvest House Publishers, Eugene, Oregon. Used by permission. **Page 187:** From *Answers to Life's Problems* by Billy Graham, © 1960, 1988, Word Publishing, Nashville, Tennessee. All rights reserved.

CONTENTS

INTRODUCTION:
   In God's Time 4

CHAPTER ONE:
   In Times of Celebration 6

CHAPTER TWO:
   In Times of Trouble 28

CHAPTER THREE
   At Home 45

CHAPTER FOUR:
   At Work 67

CHAPTER FIVE:
   Spiritual Insights 92

CHAPTER SIX:
   Healing Prayer 115

CHAPTER SEVEN:
   Renewal 132

CHAPTER EIGHT:
   In Times of Transition 150

CHAPTER NINE:
   Life Lessons 173

INTRODUCTION

In God's Time

There is a great deal of fanfare concerning the passing of one millennium to the next; after all, this only occurs once every thousand years. If you have been looking toward this confluence of time as an opportunity to begin changes in your life, perhaps this book can be the first step toward that goal. *Simple Prayers & Blessings: Inspirations for the New Millennium* is a collection of readings that will help and inspire you in many facets of your life: from everyday events to very special moments.

Prayer spans the distance between millennia and it spans the distance between heaven and earth. Prayer offers strength and light for times of doubt, clarity and guidance during moments of confusion, and security for times of change. A new beginning in your prayer life can mean a wondrous transition in your relationship with God. By listening to him, we can discover a power within us that inspires new ideas, new ventures, new perspectives for looking at old

Introduction

problems—a perfect foundation for entering the new millennium.

Simple Prayers & Blessings presents conversational prayers, in everyday language. Since there are no areas of our lives beyond God's interest, we've included prayers that are applicable for a variety of occasions surrounding family life, work life, times of celebration, times of transition, and moments of spiritual inspiration.

The prayers are starting places for nourishment of the mind and spirit—whether asking, confessing, wondering, seeking, challenging, or thanking. Sometimes we come to God with childlike innocence; other times are filled with doubt or even anger. Regardless, God is there and He is interested. We can be assured of God's attention. In the light of this truth, reading and pondering these prayers becomes like planting seeds. They are there for us to tend, and, in that God answers prayer, they are there for us to harvest.

The message in each blessing and prayer is simple: We are not alone. God is present, waiting for us to reach out and spend time with Him. Whether we are crossing from moment to moment, year to year, or millennia to millennia, God is waiting to share our experience.

Chapter One

In Times of Celebration

You will go out in joy and be led forth in peace; the mountains and hills will burst into song before you.

Isaiah 55:12 NIV

Our Prayer for Earth

For clean air and pure water; for glorious colors in sky and tree in first and last bloom, in the wings of migrating butterfly, goose, and bird. Lord of all, to you we raise our hymn of grateful praise.

For wildlife sanctuaries, open range, prairies, mountains; for backyard gardens; for corn stalks and bean stems growing tall then bending low for harvest. For your generous gifts that meet human need. Lord of all, to you we raise our hymn of grateful praise.

Every day and night we marvel at your wondrous care. Constantly you guide our choices, inviting us to creative living. All creation reflects your empowering love: rolling countryside, stark canyons, majestic mountains, delicate wildflowers, and sturdy roadside blooms. Sunrise and star, warmth and chill all declare your glory, singing together. Lord of all, to you we raise our hymn of grateful praise.

For love that gives us soul-satisfying happiness; for families, friends, and all others around us; for loved ones here and loved ones beyond; for tender, peaceful thoughts. Lord of all, to you we raise our hymn of grateful praise.

For letting us know you exist through families and friends who feed us more than enough food, who give us abundant shelter and clothing, who cherish your presence and honor your creation. Lord of all, to you we raise our hymn of grateful praise.

For the pleasure of seeing your wonderful creation; for the pleasure of hearing other voices and music; for the delight of knowing and feeling; for gathering us in families and communities; for inspiring us to stretch toward new knowledge, heightened awareness; for the blending of all experience into the excitement we call life. Lord of all, to you we raise our hymn of grateful praise.

Were there no God, we would be in this glorious world with grateful hearts: and no one to thank.

Christina Georgina Rossetti

Today: Cause for Celebration

With boldness and wonder and expectation, I greet you this morning, God of sunrise and rising dew. Gratefully, I look back to all that was good yesterday and in hope, face forward into a new millennium, ready for today.

In Thanks for a Good Day

How fortunate I feel today!
All is well.
Things are working out.
But is it luck . . . or is it your love?
I will assume the latter
and offer words of praise:
Bless your name, Almighty One!

Blessed Baby, Welcome

Bless this newborn, Lord, with hunger of soul and mind to match a growing, thriving body. This baby is born at a special time—she begins her life in a new millennium. At awesome moments like these, we, your "big children," feel your blessing wrapped around us like a baby's blanket. Give us wisdom, patience, humor, stamina, humility, joy, and grace to pass on.

How Beautiful You Are

Happy birthday to you!
That was a good day, and you were there.
Everyone who saw you thought: "How beautiful!"
So take a moment in front of the mirror:
Still beautiful, no matter how you look.
For God sees only your loveliness.
From day one.

Milestone Birthday Blessing

Bless this candle-lit festival of birthday celebration, Lord, for our special loved one. Join us as we blow out candles and joke about setting the cake ablaze, about golden ages and silver hairs. Our laughter is bubbling up from gratitude that the years are only enriching this special celebrant and that he is with us as a new era begins. We are grateful that the years are also enriching our *lives as friends and family as well, for we are the ones receiving the best birthday gift today: the gift of knowing this special person. Thank you for sharing.*

Blessed Teens

This birthday, Lord, my child becomes a teen. Surely it's just the smoke of thirteen candles making me cry. But, O Lord, wasn't it just yesterday that there was just a single candle?

From before that day to this, I've trusted you. I ask you now to bless the youthful drive to risk making choices; the struggle to be heard; the changing body, moods, and mind. Bless—and this is hardest for me to say—the urge for independence.

Bless me with ears to listen, a shoulder to lean on, and the good sense to build bridges, not walls.

In Times of Celebration

Wedding Blessing

*Bless the couple before you, Lord, with the best
    marriage has to share: peace, not of a stagnant
    pond, but of deep rivers flowing;*

*strength, not of sheltered dogwood, but of oak,
    sycamore, and beech, storm-tossed and rooted;*

*power, not of fists and temper, but of seed stretching
    toward the sun.*

Rehearsal Dinner Grace: A Prayer for Beginnings

*Welcome to our party, Lord of water-into-wine
feastings. Stand with us as we honor two special
people poised at the edge of a great venture. As this
new era opens, they begin a new life together. Be
with them on this, the final eve of their separateness,
for soon they will become a union. Be present at
their daily table as you are with them around this
festive banquet now. Be with us, too, their friends*

and family, as we share a meal, a memory, and a toast for new beginnings.

The path of the righteous is like the first gleam of dawn, shining ever brighter till the full light of day.

Proverbs 4:18 NIV

A Palm Sunday Grace

We gather this day around a table of celebration, shouting welcome and "Hosanna!" Yet, as children do in play when given palm fronds as tokens of remembrance, we so quickly turn them into swords. Take away our love of violence, our way of creating weapons from peaceable moments. And for us at this table, God of lions and lambs, heal any hurt feelings, saddened hearts, and lonely days so that we can truly celebrate being together this day in a crowd of friends and family. We have a long week ahead before we celebrate again.

I Did It!

O Lord, I savor this triumph: I met my goal!

Day by day, I reached into my heart and found energy to keep on. Day by day, I reached out and found your hand leading, your inspiration guiding. Stand with me to accept applause for our joint success.

We—or at least I—shall not be able to adore God on the highest occasions if we have learned no habit of doing so on the lowest. At best, our faith and reason will tell us that He is adorable, but we shall not have found Him so, not have "tasted and seen." Any patch of sunlight in a wood will show you something about the sun which you could never get from reading books on astronomy. These pure and spontaneous pleasures are "patches of Godlight" in the woods of our experience.

C. S. Lewis, *The Quotable Lewis: Letters to Malcom: Chiefly on Prayer*

In Good Times

Bless us in this time of good fortune.
Give us the grace to be grateful for newfound
comforts, magnanimous among those who have less,
and thoroughly giving with all we've been given.
Amen.

Blessings on the Anniversary Couple

There is no greater mystery than love, Lord of covenants and promises. We are in its presence on this anniversary day. Bless those who live, day after day after ordinary day, within the fullness of married love, surely one of the greatest mysteries. Bless them as they honor their past, even while they create a future in this bright new millennium. Let them bask in the pleasures and applause of today, when we bow before their accomplishments which, like the rings we read on the inner souls of trees, are an inspiration and blessing to us all.

In Praise of the Usual

So much to celebrate, Lord: waking to dawn gilding trees; squeezing fresh orange juice, its zest clinging to my hands all day; making a new friend, talking to an old one; watching the first leaf bud, raking the last; living to see the old millennium end and a fresh, new one begin. Each day's turning brings gifts from you to celebrate.

Grace for Advent

You are a welcome guest at this table, God, as we pause in the midst of this bell-ringing, carol-making season of too much to do. Send us your gift of silent nights so that we can hear and know what you will be bringing us this year: yet another gift of hope. Bless our gathering around this table; we will set a place each day for you. Join us in our daily feast, for which we now give thanks. May it nourish our busy bodies as the anticipation of your presence among us does our weary spirits.

Happy Anniversary

Thank you, Lord, for our marriage. Like a wedding band, our love encircles but doesn't bind. Like a vow, our love is words but sustains because of what they mean. Sustained by our love, we anticipate this new millennium with hope. In your grace, our love has the permanence of rock, not of walls, but of a bridge to moments ahead as special and bright as when we first met.

See! The winter is past; the rains are over and
 gone.
Flowers appear on the earth; the season of
 singing has come,
the cooing of doves is heard in our land.
The fig tree forms its early fruit; the blossoming
 vines spread their fragrance.
Arise, come, my darling, my beautiful one, come
 with me.

Song of Solomon 2:11–13 NIV

In Times of Celebration

Blessings for Grandparents on Their Day

They've added a new holiday, Lord, a day to honor the grandparents who tended us so well. Pause with us as we play again in the dusty lanes of childhood at Grandma and Grandpa's house. Bless these bigger-than-life companions who helped us bridge home and away, childhood and maturity. In their footsteps, we made the journey. Thank you for such a heritage and a day on which to express our gratitude.

First Day of Advent

Connected in memory to holidays past, like links in a colorful paper chain decorating the tree, we begin the first advent of this millennium. Some recollections are happy and pleasant, others sad and empty, yet each brings us to this new starting point, as fresh and full of promise as an egg about to hatch. Make all things new this holiday, even old memories, for this is the season of second chances.

In Times of Celebration

Celebrate the Word!

May you rejoice in the written Word.

The scriptures can come alive for you; only take, and read.

Discover the acts of God in history. With a new era upon us, travel with his disciples along the pathway of service. See how his church began, how it grew down through the centuries. Yes, celebrate the written Word, for it is a mirror of, and a witness to, the Living Word of the heavens.

A Celebration of Giving

Be ready to offer your gentle touch today—and celebrate the gift of kindness. Reach out to the elderly and infirm. Stretch out your hand to the children and infants. Do not hold back.

Celebrate by letting your warmth flow through. And rejoice in your ability to do God's will in this way.

'Twas the Night Before Christ: A Christmas Eve Grace

The Christmas tree, O God, is groaning beneath gift-wrapped anticipation. The table spread before us is resplendent with shared foods prepared by loving hands, for which we give thanks.

And now, as this waiting season ticks to a bell-ringing, midnight-marvelous close, we around this table are scooting over to make room for the anticipated Guest. Come, blessing us with the gift of your presence as we say, "Welcome."

A Blessing of Love

May the blessing of God fill your days. Especially, may you develop the perfect balance of duties to family and responsibilities at work and worship. As you seek serenity in these things, may you find great cause for celebration, knowing that the one who loves you unconditionally remains at the center of all your activity.

Blessing for a New Millennium

The slate is clean, Lord, the calendar as bare as the Christmas tree. Bless the new age that beckons. We sing of you as help in ages past but need to know you as hope for years to come. Help us face what we must, celebrate every triumph we can, and make changes we need. We're celebrating to the fullest this whistle-blowing, toast-raising moment, for it is the threshold between the old and the new us.

Forgiven

Celebrate!
I am forgiven!
The conflict is over.
The animosity long forgotten.
How wonderful to be set free from rancor.
How good to have a friend instead of an enemy.
How beautiful our renewed friendship.
I am forgiven!
Celebrate!

Celebrate Love

*May you enjoy all the streams of love that flow into
your life:
The love from family and friends;
The love from parents and children;
The love from pets and the love from God.
Celebrate love all day long.
For it is the breath of your existence, and the best of
all reasons for living.*

Grace for Our Feast

*We gather around this feasting table, humbled by
our bounty, Lord of abundant life; we have so much
more than we need. We confess that we are poised,
fork in hand, ready to overdo. Help us learn better
how to live as grateful, if overstuffed, children—
delighted, surprised, and generous with the sharing
of our good fortune. Bless us now as we enjoy it
amidst food, friends, and family. We give the
heartiest thanks for your diligent, steadfast care.*

Together

Bless this partnership, God, the friendship of her and me.
And remind us both: Every gathering of two is really a fellowship of three.

A New Beginning

What a blessing to have a second chance!
Grant me the wisdom to use this opportunity wisely.
And save me from the fear that I'll fall into the same old traps as last time.
This is a brand new day, a whole new beginning.
Fantastic!

Not Alone

Go in peace into a new day. You are not alone in the world. Rejoice in friendships, fellowships, acquaintances, parties, and get-togethers of every kind. You are not alone. Rejoice.

In Times of Celebration

A Blessing for Memorial Day: The Gift of History

As a new era begins, we honor those who went before us. Surrounded by a community of headstones, we remember and mourn, celebrate and play, God of history and future. We place our bouquets on overgrown graves and our picnic lunches on family reunion tables. And we feel grateful for our history written by strangers fallen in battle to insure our freedom-filled lives of safety. Our ancestors' efforts are remembered throughout our lives in strengths, names, and accomplishments that we now pause and honor.

Bless our picnics and parties as we join in the parade of those remembering, those remembered.

An Easter Meal Grace

We are celebrating today, O God, a mixture of bunnies hiding colored eggs and angels rolling away stones. Join us as we gather to share a meal and ponder both, enjoying the one and giving thanks for the other. Bless those at this table savoring the food and the message of this day. Remind us, too, Lord of unexpected appearances, that this also is the season of spring, a time when rebirth is not so surprising after all. Send us after lunch into the yard where, hiding colored Easter eggs for the children, we may understand anew what this day really means.

For All the Saints: A Prayer for Halloween

Amidst hobgoblins and pranksters, O God, we seek a quiet corner this autumn evening to give thanks for the saints whose day this really is. Be tolerant of our commercialized, costumed hoopla, even as you remind us of the pillars upon which our faith rests today. Keep our trick-or-treating fun, clean, and safe and our faith memories aware, for it is too easy to lose track of what we really celebrate in the darkness of this night.

In Times of Celebration

On the Blessings of Life

*Go forth into this new era in the joy of the Lord,
    knowing how blessed you are.
Celebrate the beauty of nature around you.
Celebrate the goodness of fellowship with others.
Celebrate the opportunity to grow and learn and
    take up the challenge of each new day.
Most of all: Celebrate your life. How blessed you are!*

Graduation Day

*Skipping up the sidewalk . . . first day of school.
Reading, writing, 'rithmetic. Frst steps, first dates,
first jobs. Hurrying down the sidewalk, diploma in
hand . . . last day of school.*

*What more can I say, dear God, than I've said since
before my beloved graduate was born? Watch over
and visit this young person with your presence. We've
done a pretty good job so far, you and I. And now
it's time to let go. Be with me. I'm better at roots
than wings. Remind me that nothing can separate
us from one another or your love.*

Help me be there for my children as you are for me, companion God. Go with this child today. I mustn't follow too closely, and I can't yet judge my distance.

For One Who Lives Well

*Blessed are you who know how to celebrate the
   goodness of life.
Blessed because you choose to see the grace above
   and beyond the pain.
Blessed because you see a potential friend in every
   stranger you meet.
Blessed because you know the darkest clouds have
   brilliant silver linings.
And most blessed because:
All you ever knew of the half-empty glass was that it
   was almost full.*

CHAPTER TWO

In Times of Trouble

I would rather walk with God

in the dark than go

alone in the light.

Mary Gardiner Brainard, *Not Knowing*

So Little Time

Square by square, we live our lives marked off in neat appointment-calendar blocks of time. Everybody gets only so much, no more, for the lines are already bulging. We pencil in commitments that spill over into tomorrow's squares. And just look at yesterday's notations: Nowhere did we get every "to do" done, every deadline met.

There is not enough time in the little squares we have allotted ourselves, O God, calling them life. We try using a larger calendar with bigger squares, but all we do is schedule heavier. Our pencils eat up our best intentions for accepting your promised abundant life.

Help us, for we want to be more than just the sum of all we had scheduled, minus what we got done, multiplied by what we wished we'd been doing, tallying up to a bottom line of regret.

Guide us as we erase what is not essential. Forgive us for the day-squares where we've inched you out; their hectic dreariness reflects your absence.

Perspective

Abide in peace, knowing that this is not the first time such trouble has entered the human race. And it is not the kind of crisis that makes a difference to life and death. It will not shed blood or cause great suffering.

Yes, it is a problem—with the one, primary quality that characterizes all such tribulations: They all, eventually, come to an end.

God is our refuge and strength, an ever-present help in trouble.

Therefore we will not fear, though the earth give way and the mountains fall into the heart of the sea,

though its waters roar and foam and the mountains quake with their surging.

The Lord Almighty is with us.

Psalm 46:1–3, 7 NIV

My Mother Died

I don't belong to anyone now, Lord. My mother died today.

Who will recall the stories of my birth? My first loose tooth? First day of school? Who will tell me I'm special, perfect, and always welcome no matter what?

Reach out to me, a little child again, lost and frightened and suddenly orphaned. I'm no more than a marionette holding my own strings, no one on the other end. Stay with me until I fall asleep and be here should I awake, frightened. Let me be a child tonight. Tomorrow I'll be strong as befitting the new matriarch of this family. But for now, Lord, find me, hold me.

In thankfulness for present mercies, nothing so becomes us as losing sight of past ills.

Lew Wallace, *Ben Hur*

Man of Sorrows

Man of Sorrows, see my grieving heart this day. Keep me from feelings of shame, though, as I let the loss wash over me. For this is a part of my life too, the life only you could give me: to learn what it means to let go.

Sticks and Stones

No matter how hard I try, God of patience and support, someone finds fault with me. I am mortified about the latest criticism. I can't decide whether to run away in shame or storm back and defend my actions, for I thought I was right.

Criticism hurts most when coupled with ridicule, and I feel like less of a person for the tone in which I was addressed. Give me the courage to confront this, Lord, for it is not acceptable to be treated this way even when in error. Keep me calm, factual, and open; perhaps the tone was unintentional, the critic unaware of the power of shaming.

Help me remember how I feel now the next time I find fault with someone. I've learned from you that there are better ways to confront mistakes than with demeaning criticisms. Such abrasive manners say more about the criticizer than the criticized. Lord, keep me from passing them on.

You can talk to God because God listens. Your voice matters in heaven. He takes you very seriously. When you enter his presence, the attendants turn to you to hear your voice. No need to fear that you will be ignored. Even if you stammer or stumble, even if what you have to say impresses no one, it impresses God—and he listens. He listens to the painful plea of the elderly in the rest home. He listens to the gruff confession of the death-row inmate. When the alcoholic begs for mercy, when the spouse seeks guidance, when the businessman steps off the street into the chapel, God listens.

Max Lucado, *The Great House of God, A Home for Your Heart*

Prayer for Between Jobs

The layoff is ice in the mind. Who am I now? What can I do? This is all I've done. The questions range the pay scale, for being laid off, Lord, is an equal opportunity ambush. As we wait to be called back, inspire us to make our job that of hunting another job. Somewhere we'll be needed again. Stand with us in the waiting lines.

Rainbow of Confession

We're stained, like a paint rag, by troubles we caused ourselves, Lord. Red, the color of lost temper and rudeness. Green, envy of others who have it easier and more of it. Blue, the shade of despair over something we could change. Yellow, of cowardly running.

Let the colors of this new time be glorious rather than harsh. Rearrange our unsightly smudges into glorious rainbows through your gift of forgiveness.

Peaks and Valleys

A chart of my efforts to change traces a jagged course, Lord, like the lines on a heart-rate monitor. Reassure me that instead of measuring my failures, ups and downs mean simply that I am alive and ever-changing. Help me become consistent but, O God, deliver me from flat lines.

Apart

Bless us both in this time of separation. May we use the time wisely to consider our shortcomings, to seek ways to amend our faults, and to reconnect the relationship with a deeper love.

Room for One More

Opposites don't attract nearly as often as they repel, if we are to believe the headlines. Pick a race, color, creed, or lifestyle, Lord of all, and we'll find something to fight about. As this new era opens, let us shed the blind hatreds of the past. Deliver us from stereotypes. Inspire us to spot value in everyone we meet. As we dodge the curses and hatred, we are relieved there is room for all beneath your wings. Bless our diversity; may it flourish.

Comfort and prosperity have never enriched the world as adversity has done. Out of pain and problems have come the sweetest songs, the most poignant poems, the most gripping stories. Out of suffering and tears have come the greatest spirits and most blessed lives.

Billy Graham, *Till Armageddon*

All One

You have said: We are all one. So when I am tempted to separate, alienate, exasperate my sisters and brothers, remind me: We are all one.

A Blessing for Failure

Bless my attempts at success, Lord, though I know many of them will end in failure. I pray that you will even bless my failures, for I also know that never risking is a sure sign of sloth and a questioning of your constant goodwill toward me. In this fresh new millennium as yet untainted with failures, I will keep trying.

Although today He prunes my twigs with pain,
Yet doth His blood nourish and warm my root:
Tomorrow I shall put forth buds again
And clothe myself with fruit.

Christina Georgina Rossetti, "From House to House"

For Everyone in Times of Trouble

O Lord, hear my prayer for all who are in trouble this day. Let them find respite in the dawning of the age.

Comfort those who are:
facing the loss of a loved one. After the wrenching grief, let their lonely hours be filled with fond memories of days gone by;
passing their days without work. During this time of financial stress, give them energy to make their employment the job of finding new work.

Encourage those who are:
finding it difficult to believe in the future. Let your hope fill their hearts as they recall all your past faithfulness;
doubting the truth of your existence or the validity of your promises. Bring wise friends into their lives who have long known the reality of your love;
struggling to make ends meet. Let them be assured that you can take care of every need, no matter how large or small.

Heal those who are:
suffering pain and illness. Let them find rest and calm as they seek to make the idle moments pass more quickly;
racked in mind and stressed out emotionally. Cradle their minds in your love and soothe every irrational thought that seeks to run out of control.

Uphold those who are:
being tempted in any way today. Especially those who may want to end their lives. Show them that while there is life there is hope, that change is the only constant, and that change for the better is so likely;
looking at all the negative aspects of life and finding it depressing. May they find joy in just one moment at a time. And may that be enough for now.

In all these ways I ask your blessing upon those in trouble. And please include me in that blessing, too!

Strangers at the Door

How can we recognize any of your needful ones we are to feed, clothe, and tend, Lord, when we see menace in every outstretched hand? Let the new era bring a clean slate. Inspire and help us reclaim our world for living in, not hiding from.

When you have no helpers, see all your helpers in God. When you have many helpers, see God in all your helpers. When you have nothing but God, see all in God; when you have everything, see God in everything. Under all conditions, stay thy heart only on the Lord.

Charles Haddon Spurgeon

Minding Our Manners

It's hard to be pleasant these rude, road-raging days. Everyone's too immersed in their own concerns to be mannerly or kind. Encourage me to get in the first words of "please," "thanks," and "excuse me"; nudge me to be first to take turns on the road, in the store, at work. Maybe good manners will be as catching as rude ones; may I be first to pass them on.

The Barriers Inside

Lord, I wish to live a long life, but I fear growing old.

I want to accomplish great things, but I fear risking what I already have.

I desire to love with all my heart, but the prospect of self-revelation makes me shrink back.

I hear the call of this hopeful new millennium, but the mistakes of the past hold me back.

Perhaps for just this day, you would help me reach out?

Let me bypass these dreads and see instead your hand reaching back to mine—right now—just as it always has.

Healing Failure

I blew it. Give me courage to admit my mistake, apologize, and go on. Keep me from getting stuck in denial, despair, and, worst of all, fear of trying again. The new millennium means fresh beginnings, and I must not let fear keep me from trying a few. In your remolding hands, God of grace, failures can become feedback and mistakes can simply be lessons in what doesn't work. Remind me that perfection means "suited to the task," not "without mistakes." There's a world of difference.

Always With Us

We know there is no greater burden than to think no one cares or understands. That is why the promise of your presence is so precious to us, you who said: "Remember, I am with you always, to the end of the age." Be with us also in the beginning of this new age.

Seeking Courage

Seeking courage, Lord, I bundle my fears and place them in your hands.

Too heavy for me, too weighty even to ponder in this moment,

such shadowy terrors shrink to size in my mind and—how wonderful!—

wither to nothing in your grasp.

Blessed are the poor in spirit, for theirs is the kingdom of heaven.

Blessed are those who mourn, for they will be comforted.

Blessed are the meek, for they will inherit the earth.

Blessed are those who hunger and thirst for righteousness, for they will be filled.

Blessed are the merciful, for they will be shown mercy.

Blessed are the pure in heart, for they will see God.

Blessed are the peacemakers, for they will be called sons of God.

Blessed are those who are persecuted because of righteousness, for theirs is the kingdom of heaven.

Blessed are you when people insult you, persecute you and falsely say all kinds of evil against you because of me. Rejoice and be glad, because great is your reward in heaven.

Matthew 5:3–12 NIV

Chapter Three

At Home

... keep your father's commands and do not forsake your mother's teaching.

Proverbs 6:20

Love-Built Home

Bless all that happens here, O God, planner and builder. In this exciting new age, may we find laughter and love and strength and sanctuary. Bless all who visit our love-built home, family and companions with whom we can grow. May we, like you, offer shelter and welcome.

Blessing a Stepfamily

Bless this gathering of what, at first glance, looks like mismatched parts, encircling God, for we want to become a family. Guide us as we step closer to one another, but not so close as to crowd. Heal wounds from past events that made this union possible.

Bless the children with the courage to try new relatives, new traditions, new homes. Empower them in their anger, helping them know that it is okay and that tears are healing. Assure them that they have the strength to live in two worlds and hearts big enough to love others. Make us, the step-

At Home

adults, worthy of this love, for it comes at great cost. Help us respect previous traditions and loves and not step too close in our need to belong. For even in the midst of celebrating, there is mourning.

Remind us to take baby steps as we become all you have in mind. Your presence will be our companion, your love our protection, and your wisdom our guidance in this awesome responsibility. Step closer, loving God, and lead us.

Children, obey your parents in the Lord, for this is right. "Honor your father and mother"—which is the first commandment with a promise—"that it may go well with you and that you may enjoy long life on the earth."

Fathers, do not exasperate your children; instead, bring them up in the training and instruction of the Lord.

Ephesians 6:1–4 NIV

Sanctuary

*Source of all life and love, let this family be
a place of warmth on a cold night,
a friendly haven for the lonely stranger,
a small sanctuary of peace in the midst of swirling
    activity.
Above all, let all its members seek to reflect the
    kindness
of your own heart, day by day.*

A New Family

*In this uncharted new millennium, we're starting a
    family, God.*

Parenthood: What joy, envisioning the future.

*What dreams for a new beginning, a new venture
    in relationships.*

*And what sadness . . . for all the free time that will
    be no more!*

*Assure us that we can do it, God. By your grace, we
    know we can. Amen.*

Refuge

As the millennium begins, enter and bless this family, Lord, so that its circle will be where quarrels are made up and relationships mature, where failures are forgiven and new directions found.

A Family Prayer

Dear God, a new age is upon us. For our family we ask your love and care in the days and years ahead. We pray for the strength to go to work every day. It's not easy to get up early and then go out to face the world. The competition is tough, the bottom line inflexible. Give us the strength to work.

We pray for the health of each family member. You know our bodies better than we do. Every ache and pain, every sickness, is a concern to you. Therefore we ask that you keep watch over our bones and muscles and every bodily system, because you are the Great Healer.

We ask for guidance in all the decisions we must make in the days ahead, the big decisions, and even the little daily ones. We acknowledge that without divine direction, our lives become meaningless, wrapped up in our own selfishness, heading nowhere. Lead us where you want us to go!

Let us be friends with our neighbors. Especially give us patience when it seems our comforts are ignored or our rights infringed. In every dispute, let us be willing to be fair, and even take less than we deserve. And give us a spirit of humility that we might offer help and comfort when we see a neighbor in need.

For the students in this family, we pray for extended hours of concentration. We ask that the days of books and classes might be filled with energy and the joy of learning as you provide wisdom and intelligence.

Give us time to play together, to have fun, to laugh. For we know that your dwelling place is a place of joy and laugher. Let us experience in this family a little bit of heaven on earth.

Finally, increase the strength of our bonds of love so that we might bear witness to your love in our community. Give us the desire to offer hospitality at every opportunity. And throughout all our days together, may this family learn to worship better and better, seeing all you have so graciously given us. Amen.

Love Lines

Motherhood is leaving an indelible mark on me, God of new beginnings. Stretch marks adorn me like a lace gown!

So much stretching goes into mothering. We stretch to make inborn nests; to free these nestlings from our flesh; to feed them. When I squint toward the future in this era just barely begun, I envision stretching to help children walk, run, and fly from my nest. Along the way, keep me flexible, stretchy, and malleable.

In your hands, stretch marks are love lines on belly, soul, and mind.

For Our Family

May your eyes look kindly upon this family, Lord, for we need your love and guidance in our lives.

This is a family that seeks to do the right things— to work hard for a living, to raise up children who will contribute to society, and to be a blessing in our neighborhood.

But we know we need your constant help to do these things.

May we be filled with love and happiness—all of us who live in this home:

by fulfilling our responsibilities, day in and day out; by being accountable in all our actions; by giving whenever we can, even when it hurts; by nurturing warmth and understanding among us.

And by always looking out for the best interests of others.

Please grant our requests according to your great goodness. Amen.

Blessing for Our Unborn Child

Bless this dear child, Lord, being woven from our love. It, too, is expanding like the body-cradle where the child slumbers, unknown but already loved. Bless and be with us as we practice lullabies and prayers, on our knees in joy and awe.

Family Resemblance: On Becoming a Grandparent

Thank you for the gift of ancestral faith. May I, as I take my place in the family portrait as the next generation, continue to keep you, everlasting God, as the centerpiece of our family, for your love is as ageless and steadfast as the wind calling my name. Watch over the grandchildren as you have over me in your special ways. Listen as I call out their names in echoes of those family prayers shared on my behalf through a lifetime of faith full love.

The Faces of Love

*Bless my family, Lord. They are a gift from you,
evidence of your unwillingness for me to be alone.
Until I see you face to face, may the faces of those I
love be to me as your own.*

A Roof Over Our Heads

*Bless this roof over our heads, and keep it from
  leaking.
But more than that, move us to give thanks for the
  next rainstorm.
Because you are more than a good roof—we need to
  remember that.
And our neighbors' crops need watering
  more than we need to stay dry.*

Good Morning

*Good morning, God! We greet you with our many
morning faces. We arise sometimes grumpy,*

sometimes smiling, sometimes prepared, sometimes behind. Always may we turn to you first in our family prayer. Bless us today and join us in it.

Telling the Family Tale

Thank you for the gift of memory. Playing "I remember" is such fun, Lord of history, especially the sharing of it with grandchildren who, like relay runners, are here to pick up their part of our family tale and carry it into the dawning millennium.

God that madest earth and heaven,
darkness and light
Who the day for toil has given
For rest the night
Guard us waking, guard us sleeping
and when we die
May we in thy mighty keeping
All peaceful lie.

R. Heber

A Single Blessing

Thank you, Lord, for the blessings of the single life.

One of your plans was for people to get married and have children. But I know that your good and perfect will is also for some of us to live unmarried and not have children.

For this life I thank you. For the gift to be free to learn to love without clinging. To seek relationships without owning, to offer my love and kindness among many friends.

Yes, Lord at times I am lonely. So I ask you to fill those times of emptiness with your presence. Enter into the barren places with your refreshing water of life.

And as I continue on this path—living by myself— keep my friends and family close, no matter how far away they live. Give me peace in my daily work, joy in the pursuit of wholeness, and comfort in the solitary nights. And please continue to give me a giving heart. For I know, Lord, I am blessed.

At Home

How good and pleasant it is
when brothers live together in unity!
It is like precious oil poured on the head,
running down on the beard,
running down on Aaron's beard,
down upon the collar of his robes.
It is as if the dew of Hermon
were falling on Mount Zion.
For there the Lord bestows his blessing,
even life forevermore.

Psalm 133 NIV

Message of Giggles

Bless the children, God of little ones, with their giggles and wide-eyed awe, their awaking assumption that today will be chock-full of surprises, learning, and love. They are both symbols and harbingers of the hopeful new era that awaits us. Neither missing nor wasting a minute, they take nothing for granted, a message that blesses us. We will go and do likewise.

Prayer is needed for children and in families. Love begins at home and that is why it is important to pray together. If you pray together you will stay together and love each other as God loves each one of you.

Mother Teresa of Calcutta, *A Simple Path*

From Parent to Parent

Today I lost patience with my child. Please help me never to do it again, God. Teach me to see myself just as you see me: a learner still discovering life's wisdom, still experimenting with right and wrong, still making foolish mistakes. And help me to be understanding with my child just as you have always been with me, all down through the years.

Calming the Storm

Bless us as we weather this family conflict. We all have certain needs to be met, certain ways of trying to fulfill our dreams. Yet each of us seeks this one basic thing in the midst of it all: love. Simply love.

Dance of Parents

It's not polite to boast, but to you, knower of innermost thoughts, I whoop and holler in delight: I love being a parent! And I am sometimes the best parent around. My children are the finest.

Just a minute . . . I must go tell them.

Despite tiredness and worry, I have moments of sheer, cartwheeling, rainbow-dancing joy. I hope there are times when you say that of me. Maybe today as I join my kids to play in the leaves, make snow angels, picnic, dance a teen gyration, or share pizza in celebration of just being together?

Take our hands and jump with us for joy!

Double Duty

I am caught, O God, between my growing-up kids and growing-down parents, and I grieve a double loss. Help me, for my sorrow, like my child-parents, is too heavy to carry alone.

Perfect Parent

When our children fall short of the mark and we parents fall farther still, O God, we scold ourselves to do it all, and perfectly. Give us wisdom to know that you don't ask us, nor do the children, to be perfect—just to be there.

Grace for the Family Reunion

We come today, O God, as near strangers gathered from scattered lives, for families no longer live close by. Be the common thread running through our reuniting as we recall and rededicate our ancestors' memory and look forward to the future in this bright new age.

Bless us, Lord of history, the next generation, as we take our place as the ancestors-to-be. Bless and guide the young ones, our descendants. Help us be worthy of their remembering.

Through this meal and catching up, embrace us and send us back to our distant homes renewed, refreshed, and revitalized until we once again join hands with you around the family table.

For the Children

Bless these children, God. Keep them growing in mind and body.

Keep them ever moving and reaching out toward the objects of their curiosity.

And may they find, in all their explorations,

the one thing that holds it all together: your love.

Graces for PBJ & Prayers for Nighty-Night

Scooting over to make room, God of daily bread, the kids and I greet you over our peanut-butter-and-jelly lunch. Bless this, our favorite feast.

Through simple graces to bless childhood fare and bedtime prayers to offer you the day, I'm honored to introduce you to my child. But how can I explain who you are to such a little one as this?

Why did I worry . . . again a little child is leading.

You are, as played back in toddler chatter, simply "dear God." An understanding wise enough to last a lifetime.

A small boy, repeating the Lord's Prayer one evening prayed: "And forgive us our debts as we forgive those who are dead against us."

Anonymous

At Home

Spice Versus Snails

Hammers. Aprons.

Which, God of everyday tasks, is the more important tool for life? Which to what child? Boy or girl?

We worry about equality for sons and daughters. Daughters are trained for grooming and gathering, for tending and nurturing—peacemaking. Sons are trained for arming and dispatching, for toughness—war.

Is this wise stewardship, Lord?

Help us tend our young ones as if all *children need* all *things to be able to build and nurture, cook and compute. Excel. Because as they grow to adulthood in the young millennium, boys and girls need and deserve the tools to be full, well-rounded human beings.*

Steer us from unknowingly forcing them into roles while the kids are in diapers. Bold, brave blue for boys; prim, passive pink for girls.

At Home

Circle of Love

It is good, dear God, to be a part of this family: circle of love, place of rest, bastion of peace.

When every other source of comfort fails, this is where I return. Thank you for being in our midst.

Bless These Gifts

Bless, O Lord, these good gifts of food and drink.

Because they have come directly from your hand, we know they are already blessed in great measure.

But may this recognition of your goodness in giving add to our joy in partaking.

Bless the Ruts in the Yard

I am grateful, O God, that your standards run more to how we're loving you and one another than how we appear. If you judged on lawns, I would be out in the cold!

Mine is the yard where kids gather.

Ball games, sprinkler tag's muddy marathons, snow fort and tree house constructions, car tinkerings and bike repair—they all happen here.

Bless my rutted, littered lawn, wise Creator. It's the most beautiful landscape, dotted as it is with children who will be grown and gone faster than we can say "replant."

Passing the Love Around

Bless us in this time of play together. Let each child know she is loved.

And let us parents recognize that the love we offer here is the same affection you have already worked in our own hearts.

At Home

For all the beauties of the day,
The innocence of childhood's play,
For health and strength and laughter sweet,
Dear Lord, our thanks we now repeat.

For this our daily gift of food
We offer now our gratitude,
For all the blessings we have known
Or debt of gratefulness we own.

Here at the table now we pray,
Keep us together down the way;
May this, our family circle, be
Held fast by love and unity.

Grant, when the shades of night shall fall,
Sweet be the dreams of one and all;
And when another day shall break
Unto Thy service may we wake.

Edgar A. Guest, *Grace at Evening*

CHAPTER FOUR

At Work

Blessed is he who has found his work; let him ask no other blessedness. He has a work, a life-purpose; he has found it and will follow it.

Thomas Carlyle, *Past and Present*

At Work

Leaving a Mark: A Blessing for Jobs

Bless our work, Lord of vineyards and seas. We long to leave a mark as visible as a building or bridge for those who follow us in the dawning millennium to see and admire. We yearn to be connected with what we do and to do something that matters.

Show us that what we do is as indelible as a handprint on fresh concrete even though our mark may be in spots no one can see right now except us. Harvest comes in its own sweet time.

Bless our left-behind marks, for with you as our foundation, our work is as essential to the overall structure of life as a concrete pillar.

I have learned that success is to be measured not so much by the position that one has reached in life as by the obstacles which he has overcome while trying to succeed.

Booker T. Washington, *Up from Slavery*

A Job Well Done

How good to get this promotion! And how I've waited for this day! Now that it is here, I thank you for the chance to savor it. A job well done is a good thing, I know. I will celebrate before your smiling eyes and give you credit, too. Because, after all, everything I am and have comes from your gracious hand.

Special Tasks

O God, you have called each of us to special tasks, purposes, and vocations, equipping us with the skills and energy to perform them. For some, our vocations send us into the labor force; for some, it is soon bringing retirement. For some, it is in full-time homemaking. For some, our vocations are in artistic skills; for some, in volunteering, helping, neighboring. Always, there is that first call from you, God of vision, working through our work to help, heal, change a needful world and mold the future in the era to come.

The Blessing of Work

What a blessing, Almighty One, to be able to earn a living for the family!

To be free of worry about what they will eat, or what they will wear, or where they will sleep.

You have given so much: house, flowers, table and chairs, even a video camera to help us remember these days that are flying by so quickly.

Yes, you have given.

And your gifts are a serious calling:

Show us how to give in return!

As I go through this day, help me to be sensitive to the fears and cares of my fellow workers. Remind me not to add my grievances and burdens to their own.

Anonymous

At Work

From the fruit of his lips a man is filled with good things as surely as the work of his hands rewards him.

Proverbs 12:14 NIV

For the Boss in the New Millennium

May you be the leader you were meant to be today.

May you find courage to temper your business goals with an eye toward human compassion.

May you carefully weigh the consequences of every tough decision you make—the effects on the company and the impact on all who work within it.

May you know that one greater than you goes before you and stands behind you, offering great wisdom.

And in this knowledge may you seek to lead just as he did: being servant of all.

Slow Down

May you find today

that, rather than thriving

on the hectic pace of your schedule,

just slowing down a bit

can be the greatest of blessings.

Out of Steam

I have lost some of my zeal to do the work here, God. Forgive me for falling into despair and for being on the lookout for a greener pasture at the expense of full concentration on the tasks at hand. Help me not to cheat my employer by only giving a halfhearted effort.

But most of all, I want to keep my eyes on you, Lord, not on things or places or the myriad circumstances beyond my control. I know that true happiness and fulfillment will come only from being in your will.

And when it is time to move, you will show me. Therefore, strengthen my faith in your goodness. For I know your commitment to me has never been in question. Your zeal for my life never cools. Praise you!

Sleeping on the Job

Achievers, it is said, spend nights on the office couch snuggled up with work. Should we all follow suit? Especially now, the start of a new millennium calls us to achieve ever more.

Lord, lead us past the temptation to sleep on the job, literally and figuratively. Grant us the good sense to know when to lock up and go home. There's nothing like a good night's sleep in our own beds, surrounded by snoring family, to get us ready for work tomorrow, refreshed and eager for your call to excellence.

Goodnight, Lord, time to call it a day.

At Work

I wonder why it is that when anxiety is such a heavy burden, we go right on reaching for tomorrow's load today. Most of us do. I am sincerely trying, though, and with some success these days, to form the habit of remembering that it was the God of the universe who said you only have to live one day at a time.

Eugenia Price, *Another Day*

"F" Is for Failure

Miserably, embarrassingly, and very publicly, Lord, I failed at work, costing the company money and time. Peers sympathize but are mostly relieved they didn't blunder. Remind me not to gloat the next time I am successful and someone else wears the dunce cap of failure. Help me separate what went wrong from who went wrong, for my efforts were well-intended. Be with me as I walk down the hall, chin up, face forward to try again. Help me learn from my failures, and first of all not to believe that I am one.

At Work

... do not depend too much upon your own industry, and frugality, and prudence, though excellent things, for they may all be blasted without the blessing of Heaven; and therefore, ask that blessing humbly, and be not uncharitable to those that at the present seem to [lack] it, but comfort and help them. Remember, Job suffered, and was afterwards prosperous.

Benjamin Franklin, "The Way to Wealth"

Seasoned Workers

Ready or not, free time is at hand for some of your finest seasoned workers, Lord, early retirees downsized, out-sized, and put prematurely out to pasture. We venture into this unknown millennium and an unfamiliar lifestyle at the same time. Help us start again, for we are hidden treasures other companies could use. Remind us as we start the search that even temporary employment is better than sitting around. Keep us in the workforce, for we, like fine furniture, gain luster with age, something young folks can't begin to match.

Pulled Apart

Like the turkey wishbone, God of wholeness, I am being pulled apart by job, family, home, errands, friends, and my needs. I'm preoccupied with what I am not doing and feel the pull to do it all.

Now, as the millennium opens, I pause to consider my options anew. Help me choose wisely. Remind me to negotiate on the job and at home for the time I need in both places. Remind me, O God, to negotiate with myself for a leaner lifestyle, for I am part of the pull. In the tugging days ahead, be the hinge that keeps my life's parts synchronized in harmonious movement, not split apart at all.

Answering the Call

Work is good right now, God of all labor, and I think I know why: You and I are working together. Is this what it is to be called?

I think it must be, for you are the source of my talents, for which I am grateful. Through the

At Work

support of others, gifted teacher, mentors, and leaders, and through those willing to take a chance on me despite the odds, you have always been present, and I am grateful for that, too.

Although this sense that I am doing what you intend for me is usually just a delicious, split-second awareness, O God, it is enough to keep me going when I am tired, frustrated, and unclear about my next step. Our companionship of call to vocation is not an instant process, but rather a shared journey. Keep me listening, watching.

I am glad we share this working venture, for on the job and off, I am blessed.

Whatever you do, work at it with all your heart, as working for the Lord, not for men, since you know that you will receive an inheritance from the Lord as a reward. It is the Lord Christ you are serving. Anyone who does wrong will be repaid for his wrong, and there is no favoritism.

Colossians 3:23–25 NIV

At Work

A Prayer for What It Takes

You invented work, God, and I am grateful.

Framer of the Cosmos, you've given me a project, too.

Creator of the Earth and Oceans, sustain my hands to do it right.

Designer of Amoebas and Atoms, give me pause to look after the details.

Worker of Ultimate Skill, accomplish your masterwork in my soul this day!

Cubed

We work on islands inside efficient cubes as small as a closet, private as an elevator, and cozy as a phone booth! Lord, give us the courage to peek around corners. We want to take down the walls a notch. It's not good for folks to live, or work, alone.

At Work

Revolving Doors

Bless the nannies, sitters, and caregivers who tend our work-a-bye children, Lord, for we leave our greatest treasures in their hands. How difficult it is to drop them off on our way to work beyond home.

Sometimes we feel defensive and guilty under the stares of others who judge our working choices. But we don't make them lightly, and we do our best to ease transitions and soothe tears—both the children's and ours—in the partings. Continue to help us choose wisely; soften criticisms, both those of others and our own.

For whether we are at home all day or not, we are all full-time parents, Lord, worrying, praying, holding our young in thought twenty-four hours a day even if we cannot be by their sides every moment.

So help us, Lord, both the working-away and the staying-put parents, to fully be involved in our children's journeys through our homes, no matter on which side of the front door we spend most of our days.

For This Moment

Bless these next few, short moments in my day, before the next problem arises. And may I remember, in all my busy-ness, that the best time to seek you is always the same: now, right now.

The Most Important Things

Bless this office where I spend so much of my time each day. In all the work I do, let me never forget my life's true priorities: family, friends, and the will of God.

The Real Paycheck

I thank you for my work, Lord. And please bless me in it. Most of all, help me to remember that the paycheck worth working for consists of more than just money. It must include meaning and significance, for myself and others.

New Direction

Life is full of trade-offs, Lord, and I need to make one. Turning to that first blank page of my new calendar made me stop and think. I want to venture off the fast track where I'm losing more than I'm gaining. Guide my search for a job where I can have both a life and a living. Restore my balance, not the checkbook kind, for it will change when I do. Your balance is not found running in a circle, but along a beckoning path where enough is more than sufficient; where money comes second to family, community, and self; where success takes on new meaning; and where, in the giving up, I gain wealth beyond belief.

Tools

Bless these tools of my work, Lord. Keep them sharp and strong and ready to do my will. And bless these hands, too, that they might be ready to do all you desire.

At Work

Come now, little man,
turn aside for a while from
your daily employment,
escape for a moment from
the tumult of your thoughts.
Put aside your weighty cares,
let your burdensome distractions wait,
free yourself awhile for God
and rest awhile in him.
Enter the inner chamber of your soul,
shut out everything except God
and that which can help you in seeking him,
and when you have shut the door, seek him.
Now, my whole heart, say to God,
"I seek your face,
Lord, it is your face I seek."

Anselm, "A Call to Meditation"

Thou, O God, dost sell us all good things at the price of labour.

Leonardo da Vinci

At Work

Blessing for a New Job

May you find your new job to be a source of deep satisfaction.

Here in this office, may creative ideas flow.

Here at this desk, may your mind be stimulated as never before.

And may all your dreams and visions for this good work come to fruition.

For the Lord, too, wants your potential fulfilled in every way.

Yes, may it be!

Making a Choice

Lord, more than half your working children told a survey that, given a choice, we would take more time over more money. And it's true, as you know from our sharing concerns and frustrations with you. We are time deprived. These days, we would be happiest taking an extra day off work instead of the day's pay. Amazing.

Are the times a-changing, Lord? Are workaholics becoming passé and is prestige for working twenty hours a day dimming? Are we going to have four-day weekends with more free time to spend as we decide with family, home, self?

Probably not, Lord, for most of us won't have that choice right away. Most of us will remain secret "time-aholics," yearning in private for more time. Give us the wisdom to ask ourselves, when this hunger hits, "more time for what?"

Motivate us to answer in such ways that will goad us to find extra time now, for even an extra hour here or there would help. Even five extra hours a week would be enough time to . . . to what? What do we want to do so badly that we will pay a day's wages to do it?

Guide our search of current schedules to see where we can pluck extra time: mornings? late nights? weekends? Taking just a little from each one could give us a sizable pile of found time to use in new ways. Help us be satisfied with this small step even as we hunger and plan for more.

Urge us to pay attention to our need for more time, for it is a worthy yearning. We need all the time we can get. And at the same time, when we find extra hours, restrain us with a gentle hand if we are tempted to squander any of our precious time doing things that seem hardly worth the effort much less worth swapping for a day's pay!

Thank you for the gift of extra time however, whenever, and wherever we gain it. With your guidance, we will be investing it wisely.

Bless My Work

All work can be good, Lord, for you can upgrade the most mundane, difficult, or nerve-racking job into one that matters. God of all skills and vocations, bless and inspire my work; deliver me from boredom and laziness.

We plow the fields and scatter
The good seed on the land,
But it is fed and watered
By God's almighty hand;
He sends the snow in winter,
The warmth to swell the grain,
The breezes and the sunshine,
And soft, refreshing rain.
All good gifts around us
Are sent from heaven above:
Then thank the Lord, O thank the Lord
For all His love.

Mathias Claudius, "We plow the Fields and Scatter the Good Seed"

Moving On

The new job waits, the old desk is cleared. Be with me, Lord, as I say good-bye to work friends. Help me find new friends in coworkers as dear as these. Help me put down roots in new parking spots, behind new desks and equipment.

Remind me each time I look at the farewell gifts I am taking with me today that nothing is ever lost, no one ever forgotten. May the memory of this place, these bonds, nourish me tomorrow; today, it is okay to be sad.

Going for the Interview

I have an interview today, O God, and feel inadequate to the task, much less the job I am being considered for.

First impressions count for much, and I may not be wearing the proper clothes, attitude, or smile, immediately losing an advantage. I may make silly mistakes, blundering through facts that I know as well as my own name.

However, Lord, with you at my elbow, I may just as likely be at ease, competent, and pleasant. Interviews are like spinning coins: They can fall either way, depending a lot upon how we view and present ourselves. Help us consult with you about that beforehand.

No matter today's outcome, remind me to look in the mirror you hold up so that I can see a reflection of someone who did my best.

If nothing else, Lord, this interview will be good practice for others down the road; nothing is wasted in your world, even bad interviews that can be redeemed into training sessions for future triumph.

Bonds

Sometimes lunchtime on the job feels like a family reunion. Our coworkers feel like family and we are grateful to belong.

What a blessing to be members of a creative, caring unit—caring about the business and those who make it happen. Productivity is up as lifted morale provides the momentum to do more and do it better, byproducts we take home.

Bless the folks down the hall, across the room, in the next department, or in the office next door. They are more than coworkers, they are workaday neighbors.

At Work

In the name of the Lord Jesus Christ, we command you, brothers, to keep away from every brother who is idle and does not live according to the teaching you received from us. For you yourselves know how you ought to follow our example. We were not idle when we were with you, nor did we eat anyone's food without paying for it. On the contrary, we worked night and day, laboring and toiling so that we would not be a burden to any of you. We did this, not because we do not have the right to such help, but in order to make ourselves a model for you to follow. For even when we were with you, we gave you this rule: "If a man will not work, he shall not eat."

2 Thessalonians 3:6–10 NIV

Fair Play

How about some help around the house, Lord, where I need your guidance to make homemaking a

*shared endeavor rather than Mom's Motel? Inspire
me with plans to enlist instead of accuse. I'm
counting on you to be at the dinner-discussion table
and in the kitchen afterward with the new cleanup
crew. Time for a shift change.*

For a Calling

*May the gifts and talents God has given become
   apparent to you in this time of fresh beginnings.*

And with that recognition,

*may there also arise a clear sense of where to apply
   them.*

A career is an important thing.

*For God's will is your fulfillment; your being in just
   the right place is the joy of his heart.*

Meeting the Challenge

May you never fear failure in this job.

Push into that fear and go through it.

Let it stimulate you to better methods

as you find new ways to solve old problems.

May you never allow the potential risk

to keep you from trying a good thing.

For this work will challenge you in every way.

It was meant to be that way.

And you were meant to do it.

Chapter Five

Spiritual Insights

Speak, move, act in peace, as if you were in prayer. In truth, this is prayer.

François de Salignac de La Mothe Fenelon

God's Will

When life goes awry, Lord, I need someone to blame so I point the finger at you. Heaven help me, I want it both ways: you as sender and fixer of trouble. Help me know you don't will trouble, for what could you possibly gain? And when the good you want for me isn't possible in the randomness of life, I know you are with me.

Most of us don't pray on a regular basis because we're deeply aware that it will cost us something.
More than time.
More than money.
More than faith.
More than becoming religious.
To lay hold of prayer as my own available resource for effective, practical, daily use—as an abiding certainty in an unpredictable world—will cost me one thing.
Honesty.

Jack W. Hayford, *Prayer Is Invading the Impossible*

Spiritual Insights

A Prayer Primer

As this age dawns, we accept your invitation to pray without ceasing. Hear us as we pray boldly, with expectation, believing your assurance that we deserve to be in your presence and to talk all we want. We are grateful that you welcome us at all times and in all places and moods.

God is faithful; he will not let you be tempted beyond what you can bear. But when you are tempted, he will also provide a way out so that you can stand up under it.

1 Corinthians 10:13 NIV

Discovery

O God, I am guilty of transgressions that make me ashamed, and I fear you'll leave me. Yet have you ever refused to forgive those who ask? Why would I be different? Reassured, I accept forgiveness and will share it with those who need it from me.

Blessed Friendship

May you come to know that God is your friend. When you feel a frowning face is looking down at you from heaven, recall that nothing you could do could ever make God love you more or love you less. He simply loves—completely, perfectly. So feel the blessedness of that!

Faith makes all evil good to us, and all good better; unbelief makes all good evil, and all evil worse. Faith laughs at the shaking of the spear; unbelief trembles at the shaking of a leaf, unbelief starves the soul; faith finds food in famine, and a table in the wilderness. In the greatest danger, faith said, "I have a great God." When outward strength is broken, faith rests on the promises. In the midst of sorrow, faith draws the sting out of every trouble, and takes out the bitterness from every affliction.

Robert Cecil (1563–1612)

Spiritual Insights

Zapped

Tree or person, lightning can topple whatever it hits. Console us with your truth that trouble, trauma, tragedy—like lightning—just happen. Random and without malice from you. Should it strike, we'll look for rainbows, assured of your presence as we pick up the pieces.

All through the Bible we see God's patience and perseverance as He pursues misguided and obstinate men and women—men and women who were born to a high destiny as His sons and daughters, but who strayed from His side. From Genesis to Revelation God is constantly saying to such, "Return to me, and I will return to you."

Incredible as it may seem, God wants our companionship. He wants to have us close to Him. He wants to be a father to us, to shield us, to protect us, to counsel us, and to guide us in our way through life.

Billy Graham, *Till Armageddon*

Running

Running is so good.

Can muscles silently praise you?

I catch a vision of life's goodness in the pounding of my feet, even in the sweat pouring down.

You made this warm machine, and you gave me the responsibility to keep it going.

I will pray now, with energy, exertion—gutting it out.

But I will not pray with words for awhile.

For you are here as I pick up speed.

And what, after all, needs to be said aloud at this moment?

God's plans, like lilies, pure and white, unfold;
We must not tear the close-shut leaves apart;
Time will reveal the chalices of gold.

Mary Louise Riley Smith, *Sometimes*

If God is for us, who can be against us? He who did not spare his own Son, but gave him up for us all—how will he not also, along with him, graciously give us all things? Who will bring any charge against those whom God has chosen? It is God who justifies. Who is he that condemns? Christ Jesus, who died—more than that, who was raised to life—is at the right hand of God and is also interceding for us. Who shall separate us from the love of Christ? Shall trouble or hardship or persecution or famine or nakedness or danger or sword? As it is written: "For your sake we face death all day long: We are considered as sheep to be slaughtered."

No, in all these things we are more than conquerors through him who loved us. For I am convinced that neither death nor life, neither angels nor demons, neither the present nor the future, nor anything else in all creation, will be able to separate us from the love of God that is in Christ Jesus our Lord.

Romans 8:31–39 NIV

Free Love

You love us Lord, not because we are particularly lovable. And it's certainly not the case that you need to receive our love. I am so heartened by this: You offer your love simply because you delight to do it.

Around the Bend

Standing at the crossroads of the old millennium and the new, I'm getting a crick in my neck trying to see around the bend, God of past and future. I'm wearing myself out second guessing. Teach me to live in today, needing just a small glimpse down the road. No need to borrow trouble that may not be waiting.

More Than Meets the Eye

May you know that a wisdom and a love transcend the things you will see and touch today. Walk in this light each step of the way. Never forget that there is more to this existence than the material side of things. And be blessed when you suddenly become aware of it: in the smile of a child, in the recognition of your own soul's existence, in the dread of death, and in the longing for immortality.

This Shall Not Pass

In this new era, may you learn to let your happiness depend, day by day, not upon something you could possibly lose, but upon that which could never, ever pass away.

Prayer for a Seeker

God grant you the joy of learning, as you seek spiritual direction in the new millennium.

Listen to those who are wise in the ways of the spirit.

Hear the inner workings of your own heart.

And grow closer to God.

Kneeling to Pray

Your changes touch my life with hope and mystery. God of love and power, I come today ready and eager to experience your power working through me.

Call to Action

We know, Lord, that action is the proper fruit of knowledge and all spiritual insight. But so often we wish only to think and muse, without ever doing good toward anyone.

Yes, it's easier to know the good than to do it.

It's more comforting to be right than to do the right thing.

It's more convenient to sit on the sidelines and give advice than it is to enter the game.

It takes less energy to tell others how to carry their burdens than to take up a share of the load with them.

But we need to be shaken out of our lethargy, God. This time of new beginnings is the perfect moment to take a good, hard look at our actions, not just our thoughts. We need to recognize that our lack of love is evident in our lack of good deeds. We need to see ourselves, so often, just as we are: sometimes selfish, often lazy.

Change us, God! Open our eyes that we may see the needs around us. Show us the poor—and all the ways we can help. Bring us to the sick—giving us words of comfort and creative means of succor. Let us no longer pass by the hungry stranger, but move us to offer what is in our hand and in our cupboard to share.

Help us to take the more difficult route of service.

Help us to forsake the ease and comfort of a purposeless life.

Help us to make friends with the unlikable, to bond with those who are different.

Help us to take all we know and put it into every resource at hand, so that action may result for the good of all.

*For if you will show us that we, too, are poor and
hungry, feeble and needy in so many ways, then
we will recognize that our giving can only spring
from what we have already been given.*

Why Am I Here?

*I come to church today, not because of duty or
because a preacher calls, but because you, O God,
invite me, your child, for whom you've been
searching. In the words and songs, the lights and
symbols, I feel, like a pulse, your spirit beating
within me.*

Mirror, Mirror

*We're too hard on ourselves, God of truth. We see
only the blemishes like teenage "zits" that erupt on a
chin instead of the smiles, the laugh lines, the bright
eyes, some of our best qualities.*

*We give ourselves depressions over who we are not
and starve ourselves into life-threatening illnesses*

trying to fit into someone else's ideas of how we should look. Which, by the way, isn't all that cute. We copy and imitate, we nip and tuck, we dye and lie.

Help us out here. What do you think when you assess us?

You say we are created in your image, which tells us something right away: We are special. You say we are salt that gives life its savor, that we are lights on hills to beckon and illumine. You say we are called by name even before we are born, that even the hairs of our heads are numbered. From the very beginning, you have said that everything you created—which includes us—is "very good."

It's hard to believe. Yet we know, Lord, that who we say we are affects our relationship with you. If we feel unworthy, unlovable, we shy away from approaching you. Too often before we come talk to you in prayer, we act like the folks who tidy up the house before the cleaning service comes.

We are learning differently, and here we are, the real us.

Bless this authentic us with our approval, for it is surely more accurate than the mirrors that fickle society, the here-and-gone-again fads, the please-love-me celebrities, and the buy-me, buy-me commercials hold up for us. All of them are selling products and images that require us to see ourselves as losers, as "less than" we are. You, on the other hand, O God, are handing out a free message that we are your beloved, beautiful, handsome, and very, very special children just as we are. Now this is an image to live up to.

Satisfaction

Comfort us, God, when we come to this awesome conclusion:

What did not satisfy us when we finally laid hold of it was surely not the thing we were so long in seeking.

Yes, comfort us by this recognition:

In all our longings, we are only yearning for you.

Is there any Duty in Religion more generally agreed on, or more justly required by God, than a perfect Submission to his Will in all Things? Can any Disposition of Mind, either please him more, or become us better, than that of being satisfied with all he gives, and content with all he takes away? None, certainly, can be of more Honour to God, nor of more Ease to ourselves; for if we consider him as our Maker, we dare not contend with him; if as our Father, we ought not to mistrust him; so that we may be confident whatever he does is for our Good, and whatever happens that we interpret otherwise, yet we can get nothing by Repining, nor save any thing by Resisting.

Benjamin Franklin, *Poor Richard's Almanack*

Weed Power

Even in our toughest moments, Lord, we yearn to grow into fullest flower. Give us a faith as resilient as dandelions pushing up through pavement cracks.

The Blessing in Your Eyes

When you look around you today,

know the blessing of seeing God

in every smiling face.

Reflect that blessing in your own eyes,

silently with a kind heart.

Oh, the depth of the riches of the wisdom and knowledge of God! How unsearchable his judgments, and his paths beyond tracing out!
Who has known the mind of the Lord? Or who has been his counselor?
"Who has ever given to God, that God should repay him?"
For from him and through him and to him are all things.
To him be the glory forever! Amen.

Romans 11:33–36 NIV

. . the Spirit helps us in our weakness. We do not know what we ought to pray for, but the Spirit himself intercedes for us with groans that words cannot express. And he who searches our hearts knows the mind of the Spirit, because the Spirit intercedes for the saints in accordance with God's will.

Romans 8:26–27 NIV

What's in a Word?

We are, as the Psalmist says, wondrously made. So much so, loving Creator, that by changing our minds we might be able to change our lives. Let us begin this era charged with the simple power of as if. Living as if we are going to fail, we often do. Living as if we are going to succeed, we often can. Keep us from being like teams who know the plays but doubt they can run them. Instead, we'll use your amazing gift of attitude, knowing you treat us as if we deserve your promised abundant life.

A Prayer for the Right Words

Thank you, God, for the wisdom to know when to speak, what to say, and how to say it. Guard my mouth today from any form of foolishness, that in all circumstances I might honor you with my words.

True Leaders

We have been guilty, Lord, of looking for our leaders only in the places of wealth and influence. We confess a fascination with power. We want to glorify the outwardly successful, passing over those who have learned to live wisely and with true integrity. Rather, we tend to follow after those who give blithe answers with the appearance of absolute confidence.

But you have offered us better, we know.

Your plan for us is that we follow those who follow the right and the good.

Your spirit fills those who walk in humility, patience, and self-sacrifice. As the millennium opens, please open our eyes that we may see those gentle faces beckoning us upward and onward in a spirit of love. They are all around us, we're certain. Only open, open our eyes!

Sunday Morning

We find ourselves here in the pew because somewhere in our lives, clearly or muffled, we heard you call. Here we are, sleepy and alert, worried and assured, certain and doubtful, to hear your message fit for us all.

Morning Prayer

Bless us, Lord, as we go to worship this morning. Look down upon our efforts to honor your name through song and word and fellowship.

And help us do it. For only in your power do we live and move. And in your being alone we find our true identity.

Sound Sleepers

Security, loving God, is going to sleep in the assurance that you know our hearts before we speak and are waiting, as soon as you hear from us, to transform our concerns into hope and action, our loneliness into companionship, and our despair into dance.

Star Signs

To those scanning a night sky, you sent a star. To those tending sheep on a silent hill, you sent a voice. What sign, Lord, are you sending me to come, be, and do all you intend? Let me hear, see, and accept it when you do.

Missing the Mark

Lord, it's hard to hit a target with closed eyes, yet I approach you blindly. Help me see that faith is not a quantity that can be measured like gas in a tank but a gift, a quality, that says, "I believe God is for me, not against me."

Silent Prayer

Bless me with silent conversations, O God, so I may be with you while doing chores, while singing in the shower, while brushing the cat. Sometimes words don't have to be spoken to be understood, and I get your message, too, in the silence that fills and comforts.

Best Friend

Know this: Prayer is quite informal, one heart communing with another, with or without words.

If we make it any more complicated than that, have we not insulted our very best Friend?

Accepted

May you know deep in your heart that God is not in love only with what he hopes to make of you in the years ahead. He is simply in love with what you are—right now—a forgiven, perfectly accepted human being.

The Worthy Pursuit

We are far too easily pleased, Lord. We run after our toys with such vigor.

We pursue every form of recreation, as if it could somehow save us.

We involve ourselves in relationship after relationship, hoping that each new conquest will give us full satisfaction.

We work and work, earning more and more money, thinking that somehow happiness can be bought, or that the joy of the future can be mortgaged today.

We multiply the objects of our amusement and the means of our entertainment, believing that if we can only turn off our minds for a few hours, our true situation will disappear into the background.

Yes, we are far too easily pleased with all we can do for ourselves.

But how much energy would we exert toward obtaining our true Home if we could only see the place you've prepared for us?

Give us that vision, God, and the determination to reach for your promises every day.

Chapter Six

Healing Prayer

A cheerful heart is good medicine.

Proverbs 17:22 NIV

After Loss, Going It Alone

Time helps, Lord, but it never quite blunts the loneliness that loss brings. Thank you for the peace that is slowly seeping into my pores, allowing me to live with the unlivable; to bear the unbearable.

Guide and bless my faltering steps down a new road into the uncharted new millennium. Prop me up when I think I can't go it alone; prod me when I tarry too long in lonely self-pity.

Most of all, Kind Healer, thank you for the gifts of memory and dreams. The one comforts, the other beckons, both halves of a healing whole.

Hopeful Night

In the midst of mourning life's troubles, you come to us. In the darkness, your spirit moves, spreading light like a bright shower of stars against a stormy night sky.

The Lord bless you and keep you;

the Lord make his face shine upon you and be gracious to you;

the Lord turn his face toward you and give you peace.

Numbers 6:24 NIV

Let Me Be a Healer

In this new era, I wish to extend my love, Lord.

So give me hands quick to work on behalf of the weak.

Cause my feet to move swiftly in aid of the needy.

Let my mouth speak words of encouragement and new life.

And give my heart an ever-deepening joy through it all.

Great Physician

We don't really know why we have to get sick, Lord. We only know your promise: No matter where we are or what we are called to endure, there you are in the midst of it with us, never leaving our side. Not for a split second. Thank you, Holy One.

The Lord has done great things for us,
and we are filled with joy.
Restore our fortunes, O Lord,
like streams in the Negev.
Those who sow in tears
will reap with songs of joy.
He who goes out weeping,
carrying seed to sow,
will return with songs of joy,
carrying sheaves with him.

Psalm 126:3–6 NIV

Binding Up a Broken World

You created your world as a circle of love, designer God, a wonderful round globe of beauty. And you create us still today in circles of love—families, friendships, communities.

Yet your circle of love is repeatedly broken because of our love of exclusion. We make separate circles: inner circle and outer circle; circle of power and circle of despair; circle of privilege and circle of deprivation. We need your healing touch to smooth our sharp edges. Remind us that only a fully round, hand-joined circle can move freely like a spinning wheel or the globe we call home.

A Lesson in Suffering

May I be blessed in this suffering.

May I know that you can use this thing to show me a mistaken attitude, a destructive behavior.

In that way, may I be blessed in this suffering, O Lord, my God.

Our Prayer Is for the Sick

Bring your cool caress to the foreheads of those suffering fever.

By your spirit, lift the spirits of the bedridden and give comfort to those in pain.

Strengthen all entrusted with the care of the infirm today, and give them renewed energy for their tasks.

And remind us all that heaven awaits—where we will all be whole and healthy before you, brothers and sisters forever.

New Math for Recovery

Illness requires new math, O God, subtraction of old fears and addition of new thought. Help me bring this lesson home as I draw ten stick figures, color the percentage said to recover from this ailment, and write my name on the brightest figure! A most deserving child, I praise you for the resources to make it happen. Sharing with you divides my troubles and multiplies my healing chances.

Bless My Doctor

Her hands are so gentle and skilled,

Her mind so quick,

Her heart so filled with compassion.

Bless her in all her duties, and in her free time, too.

For she needs physical and spiritual refreshment these days, and you, Great Physician, are the one who can help her the best.

Reflections of Light

Held up to your light, our broken hearts can become prisms that scatter micro-rainbows on the wall. Our pain is useless as it is, redeeming God, just as a prism is a useless chunk of glass until light passes through it. Remind us that the smallest ray of sun in a shower can create a rainbow. Use our tears as the showers and your love as the healing sun. Looking up, we see the tiniest arches of hope in the lightening sky.

How Does Faith's Garden Grow?

In the dead of winter, God of springtimes, I'm gardening. Carrot tops rooting, sweet potatoes vining. I don't doubt the outcome since I've learned at your knee to live as if. As if useless can become useful; as if seemingly dead can live; as if spring will come.

With Solomon, I rejoice "See! Winter is past . . . flowers appear on the earth; the season of singing has come, the cooing of doves is heard in our land."

How does a winter garden grow? With hope. It grows brighter each time I live as if, knowing that you, O God, color even our wintry days from love's spring palette.

A Blessing for the Earth

Bless the soil beneath our feet, the sky overhead, and make us one with it. We are catching on, catching up with ourselves, creator God, and catching a whiff of the garbage we're burying ourselves beneath. Catching, too, a glimpse of the fading streams and trash-strewn seas we have long ignored.

The millennium stretches before us now, unsullied. Let us live up to that promise. Bless and use our reclamation efforts, for it is a task we can't accomplish alone. With your help, we can bind up and reclaim this poor old earth. We feel whispers of hope in the winds of changed hearts and minds, for we recall your promise to make all things new— even this earth we shall yet learn to tend. We are grateful for another chance.

A New Day

Everything looks much brighter than it did before.

My prayer for strength has been answered.

My cries for help have been heard.

My pleas for mercy flew directly to your throne.

Now I'm ready to help my neighbor, Lord.

Let me not delay.

Healing Memories

How blessed are the good memories, Lord!

In fact, I am beginning to see that my happiness can consist largely in the looking back.

For that I am thankful, as I lay here, unable for the moment to be active.

Listen to what Jesus says to you: "Come to me, all you who are weary and burdened, and I will give you rest. Take my yoke upon you and learn from me, for I am gentle and humble in heart, and you will find rest for your souls. For my yoke is easy and my burden is light" (Matthew 11:28–30). Countless people throughout the ages have discovered this is true—and you can discover it as well as you cast your burdens on Christ. Don't give in to depression and despair—God has a plan for your life.

Billy Graham, *Answers to Life's Problems*

What to Do?

Someone I care about is suffering, Lord, and I feel helpless. Assure me that a little means a lot and that I'm sharing your healing love in my notes and visits. If you need me to do more, send me. I am like dandelion fluff, small but mighty in possibility.

Let Me Help

Help me to see with new eyes as I enter this new era—especially the burden of care that others harbor within them. Grant me insight to see beyond smiling faces into hearts that hurt. And when I recognize the pain, Lord, let me reach out.

It Is Blessed to Receive, Too

Being ill lately has been difficult. Having to accept from others all the time! But you have shown me, Good Lord, that unless I am open to others' gifts, I deprive them of all the pleasure of offering.

We can give touch and comfort and strength in physical healing, but for spiritual healing we need to turn to God. So, knowing our strengths and our weaknesses, we turn to the Lord because all of us carry our past hurts, and He has the remedy for everything. It's simple: If we just turn to Him, He will bring us this inner healing, this spiritual healing so we can make our lives more holy and more pleasing to God.

Sister Dolores, quoted by Mother Teresa of Calcutta, *A Simple Path*

A Little Means a Lot

O God, healing is going so-o-o-o slowly, and I am impatient and grumpy. Mind, body, or soul, this could take a long time. Remind me that recovery is a journey, not a hasty jet-lagged arrival. Bless me with faith to sustain me, step by small step. You do miraculous things with faith as tiny as mustard seeds that, in time, blossom into awesome growth. I hold that picture as I make mustard-seed progress along the road to healing.

Sunshine

Headlines tell a dark sorry tale, God, and depress us about money problems, strife, drugs, and school problems; about housing, wildlife, family, and health problems.

Trouble is so news-making we forget the rest of the story. We need sunshine to bring it to light.

Send the sun's light through creation: surf and skyline merging, bird song and flight. Send it through people: friends who laugh at our jokes, family who never stray. Send it through inner knowing: unexplained peace and joy, faith that you're working alongside us.

Reading between the lines of the gloom-and-doom true stories, Lord, we celebrate your *truth and stretch tall with gladness in the sunshine.*

Taken With a Grain of Sand

We are surprised by joy, God of re-creation, when we see despair outwitted by simple acts of love as small as grains of sand. Keep us searching, believing, and building upon them, realizing that grains of sand make dune, shore, and desert.

Present Blessings

May your thoughts focus much more upon what you have than what you lack in this trying time. May your heart lay hold of present realities rather than future possibilities.

For this moment—the now—is all we are given. Whether we are sick or healthy, this juncture in time is the place we share. Let us be blessed in this moment, needing nothing to change. Let us simply be in God's presence, just for this moment.

Support Group

This is a club no one wants to join, Lord, its membership dues are high: trouble, illness, loss. Bless all who share and support. Like your loaves and fishes, their courage multiplies and feeds all who come in need.

Ordinary Miracles

When we doubt your miracle-making power, Lord, show us the ordinary miracles of seasons, of hope regained, of love from family and friend, and of surprises that turn out miraculous simply by remaking our lives.

God the Healer

Please, Comforting Spirit, show me what it means

to let go the hope that others will be my cure.

You, Great Physician,

be my healer in this quiet hour.

The greatest disease in the West today is not TB or leprosy; it is being unwanted, unloved, and uncared for. We can cure physical diseases with medicine, but the only cure for loneliness, despair, and hopelessness is love.

Mother Teresa of Calcutta, *A Simple Path*

What Is

Today may you come to acceptance.

What is, is.

May you find blessed relief in
*　　seeing—without judging,*
*　　being—without having to become,*
*　　knowing—without needing to change a thing.*

Then, should you be healed, it will be a gracious,
*　　unexpected surprise.*

May you soon arrive at perfect acceptance.

Nourishing Tears

Thank you, Lord, for reddened eyes. Believing your promise that comfort follows mourning, we bawl and sob. In your wisdom, onion-peeling salty tears differ from cleansing grieving ones; we're grateful for their healing. Deliver us from stiff upper lips, and if we've lost our tears, help us find them.

Body and Soul

May you be healed, in mind, body, and soul.

May you come to know that all healing proceeds from God, and he cares about every part of you.

Perhaps the healing will come sooner for your attitude than for your body.

Perhaps your mind will experience peace quicker than bones and muscles.

But sooner or later, all will be well.

CHAPTER SEVEN

Renewal

Open wide the windows of our spirits and fill us full of light; open wide the door of our hearts, that we may receive and entertain Thee with all our powers of adoration.

Christina Rossetti

Renew Us

These are exciting times to be part of your world, O God, for your spirit is stirring us into vision and action to revitalize our communities. Be with us in difficult times of decision making. Still the shrill voices of opponents, for we must learn to be united, despite our differences of opinion.

Move us beyond our too-busy schedules, our boredom with routine and committees, our uneasiness in the face of change, and our preference to debate, delegate, and deliberate rather than do. Be with us as we volunteer and vote. Be with and bless us, the ordinary citizens, the salt of the earth, the "every person," for we are as needy as our streets and communities. Needy in spirits that sometimes falter and sigh under the magnitude of the task, needy in energy that is so often drained, needy in vision that is sometimes unclear.

Extend your hand of grace and bless us as we revitalize our neighborhoods, communities, and country, keeping you as cornerstone and Master Builder.

A New Day Is Dawning

We toss and turn, God of nighttime peace, making lists of "must do" and "should have done . . . or not" and wind up feeling unequal to the tasks and sleep-deprived to boot.

Bless us with deep sleep and dreams that reveal us as you see us: beloved, worthy, capable. At dawn, help us see possibilities on our lists.

Each time we yawn today, Lord—for it was a short night—we'll breathe in your restorative presence and exhale worries. Tonight we'll sleep like the sheep of your pasture, for we lie down and rise up in your care, restored, renewed, and rested.

Grains of Hope

When trouble strikes, O God, we are restored by small signs of hope found in ordinary places: friends, random kindness, shared pain and support. Help us collect them like mustard seeds that can grow into a spreading harvest of well-being.

Laughing Through Tears

Thank you for the funny bone, Lord, placed next to hearts broken by anxiety and fear. A good belly laugh is a gift from you, expanding and healing heart, lungs, and mind.

The Courage to Be

I wish to be of service, Lord.

So give me courage to put my own hope and despair,

my own doubt and fear

at the disposal of others.

For how could I ever help without first being, simply . . . real?

You have made us for yourself and our hearts are restless until they rest in you.

St. Augustine of Hippo, *Confessions of St. Augustine*

River and Sky

Move our hearts with the calm, smooth flow of your grace. Let the river of your love run through our souls. May my soul be carried by the current of your love, towards the wide, infinite ocean of heaven.

Stretch out my heart with your strength, as you stretch out the sky above the earth. Smooth out any wrinkles of hatred or resentment. Enlarge my soul that it may know more fully your truth.

Gilbert of Hoyland (twelfth century)

Blessed Solitude

May you recognize today

that not all being-alone is loneliness,

and not all solitude is a problem to solve.

With everyone far away,

rejoice in the blessing of quietness.

Fanning the Flames of New Life

Tossing leaves onto a fire, we name them as regrets and failures from which we choose to be free. We trust you to redeem even these, our deadest moments. They, like autumn leaves, can make the brightest blaze.

And now, a fresh, unexplored age dawns. Stir new possibilities into life from the embers; fan the sparks of dreams so that we may become one with your purpose for us. It is the root from which we, leaf and human life, begin and from which the most amazing new creation can burst into being, a flame in the darkness.

Transformation

May you be made perfect today—with the ability to see clearly your own imperfections, to accept them fully, and to try with all your heart to transform them for the good.

Getting a Move On

Like an itch that won't let up, a buzz of creativity is catching our attention and wanting release. The millennium stretches before us, beckoning with its newness. Songs whisper to us, wanting melodies; words and paintings are needing paper; dances, our moving feet. Help us recognize your presence in this nudge to movement.

In Stillness

I know that faith is what keeps me moving forward.

But sometimes, too, my trust allows a leisure like this.

For you, God, are the one who upholds all things.

Even as I sit here in stillness,

your breath keeps me breathing,

your mind keeps me thinking,

your love keeps me yearning for home.

Create in me a pure heart, O God, and renew a steadfast spirit within me.

Psalm 51:10 NIV

In the Stillness, a Blessing

Bless me with your gifts of silence and stillness. Neglecting to listen for your still, small voice, God of whispered messages, I talk and do too much.

Praised be You, my Lord, through our Sister Mother Earth, who sustains us, governs us, and who produces varied fruits with coloured flowers and herbs.

Praised be You, my Lord, through Brother Wind and through the air, cloudy and serene, and every kind of weather.

Praised be You, my Lord, through Sister Moon and the stars in heaven: you formed them clear and precious and beautiful.

Praised be You, my Lord, through Brother Fire, through whom You light the night and he is beautiful and playful and robust and strong.

Praised be You, my lord, with all your creatures, especially Sir Brother Sun, who is the day and through whom you give us light. And he is beautiful and radiant with great splendours and bears likeness of You, Most High One.

St. Francis of Assisi, "The Canticle of Brother Sun"

Well-Earned Rest

Lord, bless this time of recreation.

May we see that it is much more

than another form of employment.

It is a time to pull back and relax,

to honor a thing you highly value—

after work: rest.

Cheering Section

Bless those who mentor, model, and cheer me on, Lord, urging me toward goals I set, applauding as I reach them, and nourishing me to try again when I don't. In the age to come, remind me to be a cheerleader. I plan to say thanks to those who are mine.

Because of You

Lord of my heart, give me a refreshing drink

from the fountains of your love, walking through this desert as I have. Lord of my heart, spread out before me

a new vision of your goodness, locked into this dull routine as I was. Lord of my heart, lift up a shining awareness

of your will and purpose, awash in doubts and fears though I be.

By the reading of the Scripture I am so renewed that all nature seems renewed around me and with me. The sky seems to be a purer, a cooler blue, the trees a deeper green, light is sharper on the outlines of the forest and the hills and the whole world is charged with the glory of God.

Thomas Merton, *The Sign of Jonas*

On the Other Hand

I see a robin's egg hatching, Lord, and am set free from my doubts and fretting. For, while life is not always filled with joy and happiness, I know it is always held in your hand.

The Gift of Optimism

Enliven my imagination, God of new life, so that I can see through today's troubles to coming newness. Surround me with your caring so that I can live as if the new has already begun.

A Spirit of Newness

God of the new millennium, bring back to life friendships faded because of hurt feelings, marriages broken from deceit, love crushed by meanness. In the doing, hope glimmers like dawn's first sun ray and thaws even the most frozen heart.

Puddle Prayers

Pardon my muddy feet, God of raindrops and wriggle worms. I've been outside. Splashing in puddles like a child is to rediscover your creation: cloak of fog, spiderweb weavings, birds of different feathers dining peacefully together. I get too busy to enjoy it. Thank you for this mud-luscious day when I am brought to my knees in awe, the best place to meet you—as any child knows. I plan to pray barefoot from now on, curling my toes and stretching toward you, becoming like a child, as you encourage, so each day can be a whole-body experience. For it is because you are, that I am.

I Am Listening

Dear Lord, I need renewal in my life.

But tell me what you want me to be, first,

then tell me what you want me to do.

Speak, for I am listening,

Guide, for I am willing to follow.

Be silent, for I am willing to rest in your love.

Simply Sitting

O God, my days are frantic dashes between have to, ought, *and* should. *There is no listening bone in me. Lead me to a porch step or a swing, a chair or a hillside where I can be restored by sitting, Lord, simply sitting. With you there to meet me, sitting places become prime places for collecting thoughts, not to mention fragmented lives.*

There is a sense in which a man looking at the present in the light of the future, and taking his whole being into account, may be contented with his lot: that is Christian contentment.
—But if a man has come to the point where he is so content that he says, "I do not want to know any more, or do any more, or be any more," he is in a state in which he ought to be changed into a mummy!

Henry Ward Beecher

In the Dark

I know that my character is what I am in the dark,

when no one is watching,

and no one can see.

For this reason, bless me in my solitude.

Because temptation is the greatest here,

and the possibility of a setback looms large.

Slowing Down

You heard my prayers to ease my pell-mell race through life, and I am changing as I enter the new millennium. Only you could teach this old dog new tricks. I feel your companionship in walks and exercise, in contemplation and prayer. I'm enjoying this new pace you set.

Fresh Air

Today I need your help, God,

feeling the need for a breath of fresh air.

The old habits and attitudes

I've clung to for so long

seem stale and worn out.

Renew me from the inside out, starting now!

The Lord is the everlasting God,

the creator of the ends of the earth.

He will not grow tired or weary,

and his understanding no one can fathom.

He gives strength to the weary

and increases the power of the weak.

Even youths grow tired and weary,

and young men stumble and fall;

but those who hope in the Lord

will renew their strength.

They will soar on wings like eagles.

Isaiah 40:28–31 NIV

Pure and Lovely

*Whatever is right and pure,
excellent and gracious,
admirable and beautiful,
fill my mind with these things.*

*Too much of the world
comes to me in tones of gray and brown.*

*Too great the temptation
to indulge obsessive thoughts and sordid plans.*

Guard my mind; place a fence around my motives.

*The pure, the lovely, the good—Yes! Only those
today.*

Waiting

So here I am, waiting.

I have answered your call to pray.

I have heard your guidance—to sit tight.

I have chosen quiet and rest because that is your will for me now.

I am sitting on the sidelines, watching the hectic pace around me.

I am finding contentment in the little blessings that flow into my days.

I am trying to see all these things as big blessings because they come from you.

But when can I get going again?

When will I do the great works I've envisioned?

When will the situation require dedicated action once again?

When will I hear the trumpet call?

When will I finally move onward and upward?

I'm ready Great Spirit!

Chapter Eight

In Times of Transition

It is only when men begin to worship

that they begin to grow.

Calvin Coolidge

Winds of Change

Spirit of God, as the millennium dawns, keep teaching me the ways of change and growth.

Like the wind, you cannot be tracked or traced.

The breezes blow where they will: silently, invisibly, with great power.

Just as you are working in lives even now.

Let me know your calling as you move in me!

Yes, whisk with your persistent prompting through all the windows of my soul, the dark corners of my heart.

The Next Step

Lord, give me the faith to take the next step, even when I don't know what the new millennium holds in store for me. Give me the assurance that even if I stumble and fall, you'll pick me up and put me back on the path. And give me the confidence that, even if I lose faith, you will never lose me. Amen.

Trapeze Artists

Drawn like moths to flame, kids lead to us new places. Guide me, pathfinding God, for I'm an aerialist leaping from bar to bar. For seconds, I'm holding neither old nor new: It's impossible to grasp a second bar while holding the first.

Parents understand.

We can't embrace kids' growth while requiring them to stay the same. Help me teach my kids how to swing on their *bars—have standards, goals, a living faith. Steady me as I help them soar, for holding them back says I think they* can't.

No matter what today is like, tomorrow will be different. Help me, and the kids, live grace-fully in between.

Don't let anyone look down on you because you are young, but set an example for the believers in speech, in life, in love, in faith and in purity.

1 Timothy 4:12 NIV

Un-nesting Instinct

Thank you, Lord, for the gift of distance as children grow up and away. I'm ready to go on, too. My empty lap is eager for projects that will delight nest-flown children during brief stopovers, all of us too content going on to linger mournfully in our past.

Grace for Being Suddenly Single

I've set a single place at the table, O God, and am dining alone this first time without my companion, my friend.

What can we say to bless this lonely meal? What words can we use to grace this half-portion of life? Be with me as I swallow around lonely tears. Bless my remembering; inspire me to care for myself in honor of all the love that went before. From now on, I will set places in my heart for Memory and Hope, new companions for my table.

Today First

In this time of change, help me to be patient, God.

Let me not run ahead of you and your plans.

Give me courage to do only what is before me and to keep my focus on my responsibilities.

I am tempted to daydream about the future;

however, the future is in your hands.

Thus, may I be close to you in all my thoughts,

accomplish the task before me today,

and do it with all my heart.

No one should give the answer that it is impossible for a man occupied with worldly cares to pray always. You can set up an altar to God in your mind by means of prayer. And so it is fitting to pray at your trade, on a journey, standing at a counter or sitting at your handicraft.

St. John Chrysostom

Suddenly a Family

May you fall in love with this new family more and more each day. No, you weren't planning to suddenly have children, but here they are—a gift from your new spouse. A stepparent isn't accepted right from the start, so be patient. Love will grow between you as you look out for one another's inner needs. Blessings upon you and the children. God grant that you be all a family can be.

A Grace for Dieting

Are there graces for lettuce, Lord? And low-fat, no-fat, meat-free, fun-free meals? I need you to send me words for blessing this paltry meal, for it's hard to feel grateful for these skimpy portions when all I think of are the foods not on my plate. Help me change that thought, to make peace with choosing not to eat them, for I need help in becoming the healthier person I want to be. Hold up for me a mirror of the new creation you see me becoming, for I need a companion at this table.

Empty Rooms

Finally, my children all have homes of their own.

So this house feels so much bigger.

*I know it can become a cold and lonely space
  or a warm, comforting haven.*

You will make the difference, Lord.

Pack these rooms with all the good memories,

until the next time my children visit,

bringing their children, too, along with them.

Not Overnight

Dear God, help me see that aging, like being born, happens one day at a time. Calm my fears that it will overtake and overwhelm me. Help me briefly mourn youth as only a butterfly cocoon that must crumble to set the new creature free.

A Transitional Prayer

May your nerves hold out in this transition!

It's hectic making big changes. It takes away the security, the comfort, the sense of stability.

We were made for change, but we prefer the status quo. We even begin to assume that where we make our home can be heaven itself. But there is only one true heaven. And may your nerves hold out until you arrive!

Retirement

Retirement presented me with a watch that ticks only in free time. As the millennium turns, so I turn from the old working life to the new one of leisure. Guide me as I commute on the wings of prayer from old days to new ones where I'm a rookie again. First day on the job, Lord, of savoring my investment of well-earned time. Let's spend it joyously.

Students of Re-creation

Hold my hand, O God, I have a school stomachache.

First day of school.

Bless your many "mature" students and give us an A+, for we found the courage to detour from unfulfilling jobs, inertia, or life changes to answer a call to become, do, more by returning to school. We celebrate this new era with new choices.

Bless our role in your re-creation. The burr under the saddle to go, do, is a gift from you, the Creator who inspires dreams and provides resources to reach them. That's a lesson I'm excitely learning.

I stoop
Into a dark tremendous sea of cloud,
It is but for a time: I press God's lamp
Close to my breast: its splendour, soon or late,
Will pierce the gloom: I shall emerge one day.

Robert Browning, "Paracelsus"

Just Enough

In this time of great change, help me, God of tomorrow, tomorrow, and tomorrow, to trust your guiding presence. Inspire me to follow in the footsteps of ancient desert nomads who wore tiny lanterns on their shoes to give just enough light for the next step. All I really need.

Show me your ways, O Lord,
teach me your paths;
guide me in your truth and teach me,
for you are God my Savior,
and my hope is in you all day long.
Remember, O Lord, your great mercy and love,
for they are from of old.
Remember not the sins of my youth
and my rebellious ways;
according to your love remember me,
for you are good, O Lord.

Psalm 25:4–7 NIV

What we love we shall grow to resemble.

St. Bernard of Clairvaux

Growth Rings

O Lord, Bless our life stages, for they read like growth rings on a mighty tree:

our beginnings and firsts with their excitement, newness, and anxiety;

our middles, full of diligence and commitment and, yes, we confess, sometimes boredom, but also risk and derring-do;

our "nexts," the harvests and reapings; the slowing down and freedom. In your hands this time can be rich and full like an overflowing cup, not a last or a final or an empty or an ending stage at all.

You are an Alpha and Omega God, the parentheses between which we live, move, and have our being. Bless our comings and goings.

First Morning Grace

We are now one, Lord of commitments and pleasures. We greet the new millennium with lives newly entwined. Just as wind fills sails and removes clouds to create sunny days, be a constant presence each day of our marriage. Bless this first breakfast. We are grateful for it and your gift of one another.

Grandchildren at the Goal Line

Once again, a little child is leading. I had become so serious all I knew were tasks behind, tasks ahead—until the grandbaby threw me a ball to chase. There I went, like some silly old fool. But chase it I did, catching baby laughter on the air like delicate, iridescent bubbles. Thank you, Lord, for the gift of play returned to me in the hands of grandchildren. Keep me agile and ready to drop whatever task is tethering me to routine and follow where I am led, even across a goal line scuffed in the driveway dust.

The older I grow, and I now stand on the brink of eternity—the more comes back to me that sentence in the Catechism I learned when a child, and the fuller and deeper its meaning becomes: "What is the chief end of man? To glorify God and enjoy him forever."

Thomas Carlyle

Blessing for Old Age

Bless my milestones from first grandchild to last day in my own home and, dear Lord, the ordinary days between. Bless my tears, for they nourish new fields where I find joy in the harvest. Bless my aging, a rebirth into who you yet call me to be.

First Grace in a New Home

Join us for a meal, Lord, on our makeshift table of boxes and leftovers of our old life as we make a new home. We greet the millennium in a neighborhood far away from where we lived before. May your love, like the logs we brought from the old tree back home to lay on a new hearth, be the spark we need to make this move one of growth and success. Be with us in our lonely, homesick moments; guide us to new neighbors so that our daily bread may once again be the nourishing center for friends. Bless this crackers and cheese meal, Lord; it is first communion in a new start.

Setting Out

As you leave home now to meet the challenge of the millennium in your own place, may you know that your whole family will be keeping you in their thoughts and prayer. Let this sustain you in the tough times; let it keep you anchored in the joyful times, too.

Seeing you launch out on your own is so good! Enjoy the blessing of independence, and come home whenever you can. The welcome mat is out, the porch light on. And our same God will take care of you, just as he has watched over us all, for all these years.

Grace to Welcome a New Baby

The new baby sits centerpiece proud on the dining table as we eat a sleepy, still incredulous meal. Where before there were only two at our table, now there is a family eating together. Only you, Creator God, could come up with such a marvel, and we are awed even in the midst of exhaustion and newness. May our family dinner conversations in the years to come nourish and fill as we continue the creating you have begun, the making of a family.

Making New Places for God

Change is inevitable, Lord, we know.

Help us to accept: If we view each transition

as an opportunity to experience your faithfulness,

then we make new places in our lives

for spiritual growth.

There is a time for everything, and a season for every activity under heaven:

a time to be born and a time to die, a time to plant and a time to uproot,

a time to kill and a time to heal, a time to tear down and a time to build,

a time to weep and a time to laugh, a time to mourn and a time to dance,

a time to scatter stones and a time to gather them, a time to embrace and a time to refrain,

a time to search and a time to give up, a time to keep and a time to throw away,

a time to tear and a time to mend, a time to be silent and a time to speak,

a time to love and a time to hate, a time for war and a time for peace.

Ecclesiastes 3:1–8 NIV

Gone But Not Forgotten

The funeral flowers are fading, O God, but not the presence of this special one still with me in memory. As long as I have it, shared time is not ended, merely continued. Thank you for this gift. It will make bearable the solitary days ahead.

Second Marriage

Give me many years with this dear new mate, O God, so that I can piece them together in a quilt of second married love, a wedding gift from you.

Prayer for a New Employee

May you enjoy your new job. Slide into it with a calm heart. Find the pencil sharpener. Don't become overwhelmed with all your new responsibilities. God can help you approach each task, one at a time, starting on your very first day. Look to him, and your new friends, for all you need. Blessings!

Far-sighted

Give me a hint, steadfast God, about what lies ahead in this new age, for I want to see around the corner to the future. If that's not possible, help me live as if the future is now, assured that each day's grace will be sufficient.

Mother-in-Law Joke

In the toss of rice at a wedding, I've become the punch line of a joke: I am, heaven help me, a mother-in-law.

I am looking to you, Wise One, for guidance as I reinvent myself. I creak like a rusty joint as I move over to give the new mate space in my family alongside my child.

Nudge me into a gentle background role of part mother, part friend, part historian, and part wise woman who bites her tongue and trusts the reshaping process. In it, may I be a resource to call upon, not a caricature to resent.

Lord, you know better than I know myself that I am growing older, and will some day be old. . . .

Release me from craving to straighten out everybody's affairs. . . . With my vast store of wisdom it seems a pity not to use it all, but you know that I want a few friends at the end.

. . . seal my lips on my own aches and pains—they are increasing, and my love of rehearsing this is becoming sweeter as the years go by. . . .

Keep me reasonably sweet. I do not want to be a saint—some of them are so hard to live with—but a sour old woman is one of the crowning works of the devil.

Anonymous, *Prayer of an Aging Woman*

Graduation Day

Have you noticed, Lord, that we've been seeing only the back of our student's head these days? The head that today is proudly wearing the crown of accomplishment, its tassel blowing in the wind of movement into a future you both created. Today is just the next step into it.

A Birthday Prayer

God of endings and beginnings, what joy to celebrate another happy return of my day. Give me courage to face what waits unseen ahead and what remains behind. At the turnstile of a new birthday year, I am excited and ready.

Blessing New Parents

May you find that starting a family was your best decision ever.

Look into the eyes of this little one and be blessed.

You're due to receive a lot of love.

Only be sure you give even more in return.

Of Life and Risk

May you remember that life was never meant to be risk-free. And let this be your comfort in the days ahead: You are not the first to walk this fearful path, and you will not be the last. But everyone who comes and goes here is precious to the Lord and proceeds only under his watchful eye.

Looking to the Future

I know I'm going to yearn for the days past;

I'm sure of it.

I can feel the lump in my throat

and the tightness in my chest

when I think about how safe and settled I was—back there.

Why do we have to move? Why all the upheaval?

Or is it required of me so I might grow?

Don't Be a Stranger!

May you leave home with a good feeling in your heart.

Fond memories,

a willingness to write,

a desire to return for friendly visits.

You are loved here.

Don't be a stranger!

May you cut the apron strings, though, as you need to.

Growth is our wish for you.

And this is God's plan for you, too.

Receive his blessing!

The Body of Benjamin Franklin

printer
Like the cover of an old book,
Its contents torn out,
And stripped of its lettering and gilding
Lies here, food for worms;
Yet the work itself shall not be lost,
For it will (as he believed) appear once more,
In a new,
And more beautiful edition,
Corrected and amended
By the AUTHOR

Benjamin Franklin, *Epitaph on Franklin's tombstone*

CHAPTER NINE

Life Lessons

Though man sits still and takes his ease,

God is at work on man;

No means, no method unemploy'd

To bless him if he can.

Edward Young, "Resignation"

It's Tempting

In this new millennium, lead me not into temptation, O God, the daily ones, like keeping money I find, or exaggerating a headache into an excuse, or leaving racist remarks unchallenged. Small temptations, are they too trifling to worry about? It is tempting to think so, for I could easily go from occasional to habitual, from small to big. Keep me consistent in what I say and do, consistent in resisting temptations strewn before me by a world that says, "Come on, just once . . . just a little . . . won't hurt." Stay nearby, I feel a little weak-kneed.

Being Within Being

Blessed is the one who can look upward and recognize divine glory in the sun and clouds, who can look downward and be moved to praise by stones and flowers.

Blessed is the one who can look inside and find Being within being, knowing she is never alone, certain there is more to be known than to be seen.

Giving In

Help me to remember, Lord, that I have not won an argument simply because my friend is remaining silent. I'm beginning to see that I have won nothing until I consider giving in.

Help me do just that in this tough situation. I know it won't be easy, but keeping a friend is hard work. That's why friendship is such a valuable thing. And it's why I am so thankful to have it. Help me—help me loosen my grip on this one thing. For the sake of my friend and for your sake.

The Cure for Anger

O God, you see that when anger blinds the eyes the truth disappears.

Give patience for rage, warmth in place of wrath.

And wrap all in the humility that comes from knowing:

They are all innocent in their own way.

A Second Look

In this new era, give me new eyes, O God, to take a second look at those who think, act, and look different from me. Help me take seriously your image of them. Equip me with acceptance and courage as I hold out a welcoming hand knowing that you are where strangers' hands meet.

Father God, thank You for my many friends who stand beside me in all situations. They are always there when I need them to listen, laugh, and cry. They are so special to my life. May they realize what their friendship means to me. Amen.

Emilie Barnes, *15 Minutes Alone with God*

Imperfect

Only machines run perfectly—for awhile—and we know exactly what to expect from them. But we are different, Lord. We often do the unexpected, certainly the imperfect. As the millennium opens, let us accept this fact.

Give us the joy of diversity, the pleasure of indulging variety in our approaches to life. Being incomplete, we reach our hands to you, expecting help. And that is good, since only in you can we be perfectly fulfilled.

Opting for Hope

Given a choice between hope and despair when trouble hits, Lord, I pick hope. It doesn't trivialize suffering or dismiss evil, it simply trusts your promise to make all things new.

Taking Care of Today

Slow my pell-mell race into the future, everlasting God, for I am racing past the exquisite moment which, like a snowflake, is unlike any other and never to be retrieved.

Navigating Life's Rapids

Like canoeists on the river rapids, O God, we've learned that there is an easy way and a hard way to get through life. Our days are as tumultuous as any rock-strewn river, and life is as frightening as an unstable canoe:

Work—too much or too little. Age—too old or too young. Family—too near or too far. Too little time and money but too much demand. Meanness and violence making us hostages to fear. Stress, tragedy. Shifting values. A rock-strewn life.

It takes a guide and cheering family to make it through both life and river rapids. The hard way, as you remind us, is alone. Cut off from you, cut off from others, we miss the abundant life you promise. Yet running life's course as your child is as life-changing as shooting river rapids. Both require moving into uncertain waters, taking a chance on a guide we can't see, and listening for the encouragement of those we can.

Come, God of wanderers and pilgrims, be our companion and guide. Let prayer be a bridge, a meeting place spanning icy floodwaters. We sense you near and are grateful to no longer be alone, knowing that choosing to live relying on you as our guide is a move as major as paddling onto the deepest, wildest river.

Steady us, for faith, like canoeing, isn't for sissies. It is a leap, a bold intention to become forever changed by showing our trust in you. It is a loud, resounding "Yes!" to your invitation: Come, get in the boat, be fishers of folk, teach, preach, heal; be my child . . . I will guide and go with you so you don't have to flounder alone.

Accepting it, we know that you will be first there when we tip and that we need only listen to hear your directions. We feel excitement building as we anticipate the journey.

There's an easy way and a hard way to do river rapids. To do life. With you, O God, as guide, we joyfully move into the swift currents of life.

Of Love and Vulnerability

May you avoid the temptation to treat love as a mere commodity today.

It is a most precious gift, bound up within the soul of another.

It can only be given and received at the price of great vulnerability.

Blessings upon all who know it, really *know it.*

No Waiting

Will tomorrow be less hectic and more inclined toward joy? Will I be less tired? God help me, I'm not waiting to find out. In your creation, joy can be found anytime, but mostly now. *Keep reminding me that* now *is all of life I can hold at any moment. It cannot be banked, invested, hoarded, or saved. It can only be spent.*

When I was a boy in my father's house,
still tender, and an only child of my mother,
he taught me and said, "Lay hold of my words
with all your heart;
keep my commands and you will live.
Get wisdom, get understanding;
do not forget my words or swerve from them.
Do not forsake wisdom, and she will protect you;
love her, and she will watch over you."

Proverbs 4:3–6 NIV

At Home With God

Sidetracked, lost, and wandering far from the home of the heart, I long to be at home with you. Home, not so much a place as a togetherness where I am loved and welcomed just as I am, where I am sheltered, nourished, equipped, and sent on my way. And to where, when I stray, I will be found and returned. I get a glimpse of being at home with you, God, when I discover I am being constantly nurtured by an ever-present Parent.

Darkest Before the Dawn

Teach us to know, God, that it is exactly at the point of our deepest despair that you are the closest. For at those times we can finally admit we have wandered in the dark, without a clue. Yet you have been there with us all along. Thank you for your abiding presence.

Creative Thinking

Bless my mind today. I have some exciting thinking to do, and I know that all finite creativity springs from the Infinite Creator. Bless me, Mind of the Universe.

My son, do not despise the Lord's discipline
and do not resent his rebuke,
because the Lord disciplines those he loves,
as a father the son he delights in.

Proverbs 3:11–12 NIV

Hope writes the poetry of the boy, but memory that of the man. Man looks forward with smiles, but backward with sighs. Such is the wise providence of God. The cup of life is sweetest at the brim—the flavor is impaired as we drink deeper, and the dregs are made bitter that we may not struggle when it is taken from our lips.

Ralph Waldo Emerson

As If It Were My Last

Let me live my life from the viewpoint of my death, since I have been moving toward it from the day I was born.

Remind me where I'm headed!

In this way, I know I can find new gratitude and delight in each hour of the day.

For I can say: "This moment—right now—may be my last."

Glorious Failure

It is good to know that adversity makes one wise, though perhaps not rich.

And that in great attempts at success it is glorious even to fail.

Lessons From the School of Life

So far, I have learned:

Silence speaks volumes when words dry up, and solitude never needs fearing.

Giving is clearly the best joy of all, and thankfulness the goal of all living.

Wisdom will enter with force unannounced, and grace goes wherever God is willing.

Relinquishing all—this is life's success. And seeking your purpose, the meaning.

Thank you, Master Teacher! I will bring these lessons with me into the new millennium.

Longtime Friends

Longtime friendship is a two-way mirror, O God, a gift from you that returns our best selves reflected in the joy others get from just having us around. Thank you for the gift of perseverance that keeps old friendships new.

God answers sharp and sudden on some prayers.

And thrusts the thing we have prayed for in our face,

A gauntlet with a gift in't.

Elizabeth Barrett Browning, "Aurora Leigh"

Letting Go

How blessed the one who can walk this journey with a light grip on everything.

For all will be released, sooner or later.

And I wish to practice now, Lord—moment by moment—the letting go.

Lasting Legacy

Put off today and think of tomorrow.

How's that for a motto, Lord? Fine, for it invites me to forget past errors, ignore present "to-do lists," and look ahead.

What will I—family, friends, you—remember? That I did laundry instead of reading to a child or talking to a friend? What will endure? Time I gave committees instead of family and self? Chores I did instead of picnicking, walking, sitting on a log?

The answer prompts another motto, inspiration from you: Cherish the moment, celebrate today.

Friend in Need

We enjoy too much the superior feeling of helping those in need. Teach us, Lord, that it can be much harder to receive than to give. And as the new era begins, let us be humble enough to open our own hands, too, when we're clearly in need.

Speaking Louder Than Words

Bless the words I am about to speak.

And help me remember, too, that true eloquence does not consist of speech.

Let me attend therefore to my character,

for all I am speaks louder than anything I could say.

Prayer is one of the privileges of the child of God, made possible because Jesus Christ has opened up the way to our Father. God loves you, and He wants you to "not be anxious about anything, but in everything, by prayer and petition, with thanksgiving, present your request to God" (Philippians 4:6).

Billy Graham, *Answers to Life's Problems*

For a Helper

As you launch out in this helping venture, may you continually recall that charity begins, but does not end, at home. That is why you are going.

When you seem to lose all your energy, when you've given all you can, rest in God's strength. When you come to the end of your rope, and patience seems to fly away, settle back in God's waiting arms.

Make times of peace and quiet for yourself!

And when you feel as though you'd like to quit and go home, persevere in the light of God's long-standing love for you over the years.

In all this hard work, rely not on your own willpower, but discover the blessing of being weak and in need. For this is the only way you will succeed, and it is the only way for others to have the opportunity to do something kind for you. Along with them—be blessed!

The text: Love thou thy fellow man!
  He may have sinned, One proof indeed,
He is thy fellow, reach thy hand
  And help him in his need!

Love thou thy fellow man. He may
  Have wronged thee—then, the less excuse.
Thou hast for wronging him. Obey
  What he has dared refuse!

Love thou thy fellow man—for, be
  His life a light or heavy load,
No less he needs the love of thee
  To help him on his road.

James Whitcomb Riley, "The Text"

Check It Out

It might be something, it might be nothing. Silly, silly us, ostriches with heads in the sand, we put off finding out. Remind us that the lives we gamble are gifts from you. Be with us as we check it out and check off worries that are probably nothing at all.

Balanced Diet

In these nutrition infomercial, edutainment times, prepare me a table of pleasurable moderation. And, Lord of salads and sundaes, assure that nothing in your creation is itself bad; as always, it's what I do with it that determines its value. Be with me at the smorgasbord.

Eeny Meeny

I could flip a coin, Lord, and make a decision as sensibly as if I heeded the advice being peddled. Experts expound on both sides of every issue, food to seat belts, and change their minds by tomorrow. Help me not do myself in by ignoring all of it! Moderation, Lord, moderation—I hear you.

Different Is Lovely

We want to belong and go to great lengths to fit anonymously in, forgetting we are like snowflakes, no two, thank God, alike. Each, snowflake and child of yours, is the same in essence but different in form. Bless our one-of-a-kind value. We are heartened to know that no one is created more special. It is not your way to be unnatural, to make one snowflake better than another.

Over mountains
and over valleys
and over oceans
and over rivers
and over deserts
one says: Blessed are You, Lord, our God, king of the world, who makes the works of creation. . . .

Over rain
and over good news
one says: Blessed are You, Lord, our God, ruler of the world, who is God and who does good things.

And for bad news
one says: Blessed are You, Lord, our God, ruler of the world, who is the true judge.

The Talmud, Blessings, Berakhot 9:2

Beautiful

You said that I am worthwhile and beautiful, Lord.

I hardly believed it

until one of your children—just this morning—

told me the same.

Extreme Love

You are everywhere, Lord, and we're comforted to be enfolded as we move through life's extremes. You are with us in birthings and dyings, in routine and surprise, and in stillness and activity. You are with us as we venture into the unexplored new millennium. We cannot wander so far in any direction that you are not already there.